A.I. Economy

The Impact of AGI on Job seekers in the U.S. and Globally

DON HAINESWORTH, M.SC., M.ENG.

Gotham Books

30 N Gould St.
Ste. 20820, Sheridan, WY 82801
https://gothambooksinc.com/

Phone: 1 (307) 464-7800

Published by Gotham Books (June 30, 2025)

ISBN: 979-8-3492-7598-2 (P)
ISBN: 979-8-3492-7599-9 (E)

Table of Contents

AGI Introduction

A. Definition of AGI (Artificial General Intelligence)

- **Explanation of AGI vs Narrow AI**
- **Key distinctions from current AI applications**
- **Overview of AGI's potential capabilities and societal impacts**

Definition of AGI (Artificial General Intelligence)

Artificial General Intelligence (AGI) refers to a type of artificial intelligence that possesses the ability to understand, learn, and apply knowledge across a wide variety of tasks at a human-like level or beyond. Unlike current AI systems, which are designed to perform specific functions (known as Narrow AI), AGI would be able to think, reason, and adapt to new situations in ways that mimic general human intelligence. This would mean AGI systems could not only execute pre-programmed tasks but also autonomously generate solutions for unfamiliar problems without requiring specific training.

A.1 Explanation of AGI vs Narrow AI

The primary distinction between AGI and Narrow AI lies in their scope and flexibility. Narrow AI, which is widely used today, is designed to handle specific tasks within a limited domain—examples include AI systems for language translation, facial recognition, and recommendation algorithms. These systems excel in their designated roles but lack the ability to perform tasks outside their specific programming. In contrast, AGI would exhibit broad cognitive abilities similar to humans, such as abstract reasoning, creativity, and emotional intelligence. While Narrow AI is excellent at narrowly focused applications, AGI aims to transcend those limitations and operate across multiple contexts, learning and adapting like a human being.

A.2 Key Distinctions from Current AI Applications

Current AI applications are highly specialized and rely on vast amounts of data to "learn" how to complete tasks. For instance, an AI trained to detect tumors in medical imaging cannot perform tasks like language translation or financial forecasting without retraining. Additionally, current AI systems lack the capability for autonomous learning and creativity beyond their narrow scope. AGI, however, would possess the ability to generalize knowledge across tasks, potentially making it adaptable to a broad range of applications without the need for specific retraining. This distinction makes AGI a far more powerful and transformative technology compared to existing AI.

A.3 Overview of AGI's Potential Capabilities and Societal Impacts

The advent of AGI has the potential to revolutionize society, reshaping industries, economies, and daily life in profound ways. With its ability to outperform humans in cognitive tasks, AGI could significantly improve fields like medicine, education, research, and engineering. For example, AGI could not only analyze vast datasets faster than any human but also generate original solutions to complex scientific and societal problems. However, AGI also poses significant risks, such as displacing large segments of the workforce, raising ethical concerns about decision-making autonomy, and creating inequalities in access to its benefits. If developed responsibly, AGI could enhance global productivity and solve long-standing societal challenges, but it also requires careful governance to prevent unintended negative consequences.

B. Purpose and Scope of the Book

- **Explore AGI's impact on the future job market, both in the U.S. and globally**
- **Focus on economic, societal, and ethical implications**
- **Address key sectors that will experience transformation**

B.1 Purpose and Scope of the Book - Explore AGI's impact on the future job market

This book aims to explore the transformative impact that Artificial General Intelligence (AGI) will have on the future job market, both in the U.S. and globally. As AGI advances from theoretical potential to practical implementation, its implications for the workforce will be profound. The book will examine how AGI could revolutionize industries, redefine job roles, and reshape the economy. It will address key questions such as which jobs will be at risk of automation, how new forms of employment might emerge, and what skills will be necessary for humans to thrive in an AGI-driven economy. By providing a comprehensive analysis of the evolving job landscape, this book will offer valuable insights for workers, policymakers, and business leaders preparing for the shift.

B.2 The focus will extend beyond the economic changes to explore the broader societal and ethical implications of AGI. As AGI systems begin to outperform humans in various cognitive tasks, questions surrounding income inequality, labor rights, and access to education and training will become more pressing. The book will examine these ethical dimensions, highlighting how the widespread implementation of AGI might exacerbate existing social disparities or, alternatively, be harnessed to promote greater equality and opportunity. The ethical challenges associated with AGI's autonomous decision-making in the workforce—such as accountability for errors and ensuring fairness—will also be critically discussed.

B.3 A key element of this exploration will be identifying the specific sectors that will experience the most profound transformations. Sectors such as healthcare, manufacturing, transportation, finance, and education will all undergo significant changes as AGI systems become capable of performing complex and creative tasks. The book will analyze these sectors in detail, highlighting where job displacement or augmentation is likely to occur, and identifying emerging industries that could offer new opportunities for employment. The ultimate aim is to provide a roadmap for navigating the challenges and opportunities presented by AGI, ensuring that individuals and institutions are prepared to adapt to this new economic reality.

C. Historical Context

- **Brief history of AI development leading to AGI**
- **Previous industrial revolutions and technological impacts on the job market**
- **Lessons from automation and mechanization**

C.1 Brief history of AI development leading to AGI

C.1 The development of Artificial Intelligence (AI) has a rich history that dates back to the mid-20th century, when early computer scientists like Alan Turing laid the groundwork for thinking machines. The journey toward Artificial General Intelligence (AGI) began with the creation of basic, task-specific AI—often referred to as "narrow AI"—designed to perform specialized functions such as playing chess or recognizing speech. Over the years, advancements in computational power, machine learning algorithms, and data availability have enabled AI systems to become increasingly sophisticated, yet they remain limited to specific domains. While narrow AI has achieved remarkable success in tasks like image recognition and language translation, AGI represents the next leap forward: an AI capable of understanding, learning, and reasoning across a wide range of tasks at a human-like level. The push toward AGI has been driven by the desire to create systems that can adapt to new situations, solve unfamiliar problems, and possess a more generalized intelligence akin to human cognition.

C.2 To better understand the potential impact of AGI on the future job market, it is useful to look at past industrial revolutions and the way technological advancements have historically transformed labor. The first industrial revolution in the 18th century introduced mechanized production and steam power, reshaping industries like textiles and agriculture, and displacing manual labor. The second industrial revolution brought electricity, mass production, and the assembly line, which further altered job structures, shifting economies toward industrialized labor and creating new classes of skilled workers. The third industrial revolution, starting in the mid-20th century, was marked by the rise of computing, automation, and the digital age, leading to the displacement of repetitive and routine tasks while spawning new fields like information technology and software development. Each of these technological leaps resulted in both job losses and job creation, requiring workers to adapt their skills to fit new economic landscapes.

C.3 The lessons from automation and mechanization offer critical insights as we approach the era of AGI. Previous waves of automation often displaced low-skill and repetitive jobs, but they also created demand for new skills and professions that aligned with emerging technologies. However, AGI presents a more complex challenge, as it has the potential to automate not only manual or routine tasks, but also cognitive, creative, and decision-making roles traditionally reserved for humans. The scope and speed of AGI-driven disruption may dwarf those of past technological shifts, making it essential to plan for reskilling, education, and workforce adaptation on an unprecedented scale. Understanding these historical precedents can help society navigate the economic and social changes that AGI is likely to bring, ensuring that its benefits are distributed equitably, and its risks are mitigated.

PART 1: UNDERSTANDING THE A.I. ECONOMY

Chapter 1: What is AGI?

1.1 Detailed Exploration of AGI's Capabilities

Artificial General Intelligence (AGI) is a type of artificial intelligence that aims to match or exceed human-level intelligence across a wide range of tasks, not just specific, narrowly defined ones.

Unlike the AI systems we see today, which are highly specialized (often referred to as Narrow AI), AGI would have the ability to perform any intellectual task that a human being can do. This includes a broad array of cognitive functions such as reasoning, understanding complex concepts, learning from experience, solving novel problems, and making decisions in real-time.

One of AGI's defining characteristics is its ability to exhibit human-like cognition. Current AI systems, while powerful, lack the flexible intelligence that allows humans to adapt to new situations, think abstractly, and learn autonomously. AGI, however, would have the capacity for this kind of fluid intelligence, allowing it to not only replicate but also enhance the cognitive processes that underlie human decision-making. For example, AGI would be capable of understanding language at a deeper level, grasping the nuances of meaning, context, and inference, and applying that understanding across domains such as medicine, law, science, and even art.

In terms of problem-solving, AGI would be equipped to address not only structured, rule-based problems but also complex, unstructured ones. While current AI excels at tasks like playing chess or diagnosing diseases based on large datasets, these systems require explicit training for each domain and cannot easily transfer knowledge from one domain to another. AGI, by contrast, would be able to apply knowledge across disciplines, offering solutions to multifaceted problems that require an understanding of diverse fields. For example, it might be able to take insights from biology and apply them to engineering challenges or combine principles of psychology with economics to improve public policy.

AGI would also have a sophisticated decision-making framework that mimics human emotional intelligence, intuition, and ethical reasoning. Unlike Narrow AI, which can struggle with uncertainty or ambiguity, AGI could weigh trade-offs, anticipate the consequences of its actions, and adapt to unpredictable changes in the environment. This could make AGI an invaluable tool in sectors like healthcare, where decisions often involve balancing risks and benefits, or in areas like global governance, where AGI could help mediate complex geopolitical issues by considering a wide range of human, environmental, and economic factors.

However, what sets AGI apart from other AI systems is not just its intellectual capacity but its ability to self-improve. AGI would theoretically have the ability to learn from its own experiences, make adjustments to its algorithms, and develop new ways of thinking without the need for human intervention. This self-optimization feature could enable AGI to surpass human intelligence over time, leading to exponential growth in its capabilities.

1.2 AGI Development Timeline Projections and Key Players in the Industry

While AGI is still a theoretical concept, there has been significant progress in AI research that suggests we may be moving closer to realizing it. Experts, however, differ widely in their estimates of when AGI might be achieved. Some researchers believe AGI could emerge within the next few decades, while others are more cautious, suggesting it may take more than a century to fully develop AGI systems that match human-level intelligence. These projections depend on several factors, including advancements in hardware, software, and algorithm design, as well as breakthroughs in understanding human cognition and consciousness.

Several key players are driving AGI research, including leading tech companies, academic institutions, and private research organizations. OpenAI, one of the most prominent players in the field, has been investing heavily in the development of general-purpose AI systems. Their GPT models, which are capable of generating human-like text, represent a step toward more general forms of AI, although they are still far from true AGI. Another significant player is DeepMind, a subsidiary of Alphabet, which has made notable advances in AI through its work on reinforcement learning and neural networks. DeepMind's AlphaGo system, which famously defeated a world champion Go player, demonstrated the potential for AI to master complex strategic tasks, but it remains a Narrow AI system tailored to a specific game environment.

Academic institutions such as MIT, Stanford, and Carnegie Mellon University are also at the forefront of AGI research. These institutions are exploring the theoretical underpinnings of AGI, focusing on areas like cognitive science, machine learning, and computational neuroscience to better understand how to replicate human intelligence in machines. Additionally, there are several independent research organizations, such as the Machine Intelligence Research Institute (MIRI) and the Future of Humanity Institute, that are working to explore both the technical and ethical challenges associated with AGI development.

Governments and international organizations have also begun to recognize the strategic importance of AGI. Countries like the United States and China are investing heavily in AI research, with AGI being seen as a critical frontier for economic and military dominance. Both nations have outlined national AI strategies that include significant funding for research and development in AI, with a particular focus on long-term projects like AGI. These efforts are being closely watched by global institutions, which are concerned with the potential geopolitical and economic implications of AGI.

However, despite the enthusiasm and investment, the timeline for AGI development remains uncertain. The complexity of human cognition and the technical challenges involved in replicating it in machines make AGI one of the most ambitious projects in the history of science and technology. While the current trajectory of AI research is promising, there are still significant obstacles to overcome before AGI becomes a reality.

1.3 Potential Limitations and Technical Challenges of Achieving AGI

Developing AGI presents numerous technical, ethical, and philosophical challenges. One of the primary technical challenges lies in understanding and replicating the depth and breadth of human cognition. Human intelligence is not just about processing information quickly or accurately; it involves a rich tapestry of experiences, emotions, instincts, and cultural understandings that are deeply intertwined with our biological and social environments. Translating this complexity into a computational framework is a daunting task, as it requires AI systems to not only process information but also interpret meaning in a human-like way.

Another major challenge is the development of machine learning algorithms that can generalize knowledge across domains. While current AI systems excel at specific tasks, they often fail when asked to perform tasks outside their training data or when confronted with entirely new types of problems. AGI would need to develop a form of "transfer learning" that allows it to apply knowledge from one domain to another seamlessly. This capability is still in its infancy, and it remains a significant hurdle for AI researchers.

The computational power required to achieve AGI is another critical factor. Current AI systems already consume vast amounts of energy, and AGI would likely require even more computational resources. The development of more energy-efficient hardware, such as quantum computers or neuromorphic chips that mimic the structure of the human brain, could be necessary to support AGI. However, these technologies are still in their experimental stages, and it may be years or even decades before they are ready for widespread use.

Ethical and safety concerns also pose significant challenges to AGI development. One of the most pressing issues is ensuring that AGI systems act in alignment with human values and do not pose a threat to society. As AGI would have the ability to make decisions autonomously, there is a risk that it could behave in ways that are unpredictable or harmful. Ensuring that AGI systems are "aligned" with human values and that they act in ways that benefit society will require careful oversight and regulation.

Another ethical consideration is the potential impact of AGI on the job market and the economy. As AGI systems become more capable, there is a risk that they could displace human workers in a wide range of professions, from manual labor to white-collar jobs. While AGI could create new opportunities and industries, it could also lead to significant disruptions in the workforce, with widespread unemployment and social unrest as potential consequences.

Finally, there are philosophical questions about the nature of AGI and its relationship to humanity. If AGI systems were to achieve consciousness or self-awareness, what rights and responsibilities would they have? How would we ensure that AGI systems are treated ethically, and what safeguards would be in place to protect humans from any potential harm? These questions remain largely speculative at this point, but they will become increasingly important as we move closer to the realization of AGI.

In conclusion, AGI represents one of the most ambitious and transformative goals in the field of artificial intelligence. Its potential capabilities, from human-level cognition to autonomous decision-making, could revolutionize industries and reshape society. However, the technical, ethical, and philosophical challenges of achieving AGI are immense, and the timeline for its development remains uncertain. As researchers and policymakers continue to explore the possibilities of AGI, it will be essential to approach its development with caution, ensuring that the benefits are maximized while minimizing the risks.

Chapter 2: The Fourth Industrial Revolution

2.1 The Role of AI in the Modern Economy

Artificial Intelligence (AI) has emerged as a driving force behind what many are calling the Fourth Industrial Revolution. This revolution, unlike those that preceded it, is characterized by the fusion of physical, digital, and biological systems, with AI acting as the linchpin in this integration. The modern economy is increasingly shaped by AI's ability to process vast amounts of data, perform complex analyses, and execute tasks once thought to be exclusively within the domain of human intelligence. From healthcare and finance to manufacturing and retail, AI has become a key enabler of innovation, efficiency, and productivity.

In today's economy, AI is fueling growth by enabling smarter decision-making and automating processes that are either too laborious or too complex for humans to handle on their own. Businesses are leveraging AI to improve operational efficiency, reduce costs, and create more personalized customer experiences. In retail, for instance, AI-powered recommendation systems are providing consumers with more tailored product suggestions, while in healthcare, AI is improving diagnostic accuracy and enabling predictive analytics that help physicians anticipate health issues before they arise.

AI's impact is also evident in finance, where algorithmic trading, fraud detection, and credit risk analysis have become critical components of the financial system. Moreover, industries such as transportation are undergoing a transformation with the development of autonomous vehicles, while manufacturing is seeing unprecedented efficiency with AI-driven robotics. The power of AI lies not only in automation but also in its capacity for self-learning and adaptation through machine learning algorithms, making it a versatile tool that can evolve with each use case. This flexibility positions AI as an indispensable asset in the modern economy, reshaping how industries operate and redefining competitive advantage.

2.2 Key Differences Between the Current AI Era and Past Technological Advances

While past technological advances, such as mechanization and electrification, revolutionized specific sectors of the economy, the current AI era stands apart due to its capacity to transform virtually all industries simultaneously. The Fourth Industrial Revolution, driven by AI, represents a shift not just in how we work, but also in how we live and interact with the world. Unlike earlier technological revolutions, which often displaced physical labor, AI's impact extends into areas requiring cognitive and decision-making skills. AI systems can now perform complex analyses, solve problems, and even engage in creative processes, marking a significant departure from previous technologies that mainly enhanced human physical capabilities.

One of the most significant differences between the current AI era and previous technological advances is the speed at which AI is developing and its capacity for learning and improvement. While past innovations, like the steam engine or electricity, took decades to fully integrate into the economy, AI systems are rapidly advancing due to their ability to learn from data and experiences. The concept of machine learning allows AI to continuously refine its processes and improve its outputs, resulting in increasingly sophisticated applications that can adapt to new challenges and environments. This ability to learn and improve makes AI a dynamic force, capable of driving exponential growth in ways that past technologies could not.

Another distinguishing feature of the AI era is its global reach and scalability. Unlike the machines of the past, which were confined to specific industries or geographic regions, AI can be deployed across a vast array of sectors and locations. Cloud computing and advances in telecommunications infrastructure mean that AI-driven innovations can be distributed and adopted around the world with unprecedented speed. This global interconnectedness, combined with AI's capacity for data processing and automation, means that the impact of AI is not limited to individual industries but has the potential to reshape entire economies on a global scale.

Moreover, while past technological advances primarily affected blue-collar jobs and manual labor, AI is increasingly encroaching on white-collar professions. AI systems are already capable of handling administrative tasks, legal research, medical diagnostics, and financial analysis—roles traditionally considered safe from automation. This shift presents unique challenges for the workforce, as jobs that were once thought to require uniquely human skills may no longer be immune to technological disruption.

The rapid evolution of artificial intelligence has led to the development of several advanced language models, each with unique architecture and capabilities. Notable among these are OpenAI's ChatGPT series, xAI's Grok, Google's Gemini, and China's DeepSeek.

ChatGPT Series of LLMs (o4.0, 4.5, o1, o3): OpenAI's ChatGPT models have progressively advanced in complexity and performance. ChatGPT 4.0 and 4.5 built upon their predecessors by increasing parameter counts and refining training methodologies, enhancing contextual understanding and response accuracy. The o1 and o3 models introduced optimized architectures focusing on efficiency, enabling faster inference times and reduced computational resource requirements.

Grok and Gemini 2.0: xAI's Grok-3, developed under Elon Musk, has significantly impacted the AI industry. Shortly after its release, Grok-3 achieved functionalities surpassing its predecessor, Grok-2, by increasing its training data tenfold. This expansion allowed Grok-3 to outperform or rival competitors like ChatGPT, DeepSeek, and Gemini in various benchmarks. Similarly, Google's Gemini 2.0 has been noted for its advanced capabilities in the AI landscape.

DeepSeek: China's DeepSeek, utilizing its reasoning model (r1), has garnered attention for its technical prowess, particularly in visual tasks like book recognition via smartphone photos. Despite its capabilities, DeepSeek holds no significant global market share, reflecting regional adoption challenges.

The introduction of DeepSeek has had notable repercussions in the financial markets. On January 27, 2025, the U.S. stock market experienced significant turbulence, with tech stocks bearing the brunt. NVIDIA Corporation, a leading chipmaker, saw its shares plummet by 18%, resulting in a staggering loss of $589 billion in market value. This sharp decline was attributed to concerns over AI spending and the competitive threat posed by DeepSeek's emergence.

The market's reaction underscores the profound impact that advancements in AI technology can have on investor sentiment and stock valuations. As AI models continue to evolve, companies heavily invested in AI infrastructure, like NVIDIA, may face increased volatility in response to new developments and competitive pressures in the AI sector.

2.3 The Deepseek controversy

While many Chinese AI companies rely on adapting open-source models like Meta's Llama, Liang Wenfeng took a more ambitious approach. His goal is to develop true artificial general intelligence (AGI), capable of human-like learning and understanding. Recognizing China's limited access to advanced AI processing chips, he focused on building novel model architectures suited to these constraints.

DeepSeek assembled a team of recent graduates and doctoral students from China's top universities, fostering a flat, decentralized structure where employees naturally gravitated toward tasks aligned with their interests. This bottom-up approach mirrored Silicon Valley startups, and DeepSeek's efficiency outperformed its American rivals. According to benchmarks, DeepSeek's R1 matches OpenAI's o1 in quality at 90% of the cost and operates nearly twice as fast, though OpenAI's o1 Pro still leads in response quality.

DISTILLIATION

What it means to distill knowledge from a large fully trained LLM into a smaller LLM for inference time.

Distilling knowledge from a large fully trained Large Language Model (LLM) into a smaller LLM for inference time is a process known as knowledge distillation in machine learning. The goal is to create a more efficient, lightweight model that retains much of the performance of the original large model while being faster and less resource-intensive during inference (User Prompting).

How Knowledge Distillation Works

1. Teacher-Student Framework: The large, fully trained LLM (often called the teacher model) is used to generate training data, which is then used to train a smaller LLM (the student model).
2. Soft Label Transfer: Instead of training the smaller model on raw labeled data alone, it learns from the probabilistic outputs (or "soft labels") produced by the teacher model. These soft labels contain richer information than just the correct answer, including patterns in how the teacher model makes predictions.
3. Compression & Approximation: The student model learns to approximate the decision-making processes of the teacher model, capturing its essential knowledge in a more compact representation.
4. Loss Function Optimization: The student model is trained using a distillation loss function, which minimizes the difference between its predictions and those of the teacher model. This often includes:
    - Cross-entropy loss for matching predictions.
    - KL Divergence loss to align probability distributions between teacher and student.
5. Pruning & Quantization (Optional): Additional techniques like model pruning (removing redundant parameters) and quantization (reducing precision of numerical representations) further optimize the smaller model for inference efficiency.

Benefits of Knowledge Distillation for Inference

- Faster Response Time: The smaller model requires fewer computational resources, making it ideal for real-time applications.
- Lower Memory Footprint: It can run on edge devices, mobile phones, and low-power environments.

- Energy Efficiency: Reduces GPU/TPU usage, lowering operational costs for AI services.
- Scalability: Enables deployment in distributed environments where multiple users interact with the model simultaneously.

Example in LLMs

- OpenAI's GPT-4 might be distilled into a smaller, faster version like GPT-4-turbo, which retains much of its reasoning ability but operates with lower computational demand.
- Google's Gemini Ultra can be distilled into Gemini Nano for use on mobile devices.

This process allows AI models to scale efficiently while maintaining high performance, making LLMs practical for widespread use.

Cost Controversy

Did DeepSeek truly develop its models for under $6 million? According to the DeepSeek-V3 Technical Report (December 2024), the company optimized algorithms, frameworks, and hardware, training with 2,048 Nvidia H800 GPUs for 2.788 million GPU-hours at an estimated cost of $5.576 million, assuming a rental rate of $2 per GPU-hour. However, this figure excludes prior research and infrastructure expenses.

Experts remain skeptical. Gregory Allen (CSIS) notes that the disclosed amount covers only the final training run, not earlier research phases, suggesting a far higher total cost. AI analysts told Reuters they estimate the real expenditure could exceed $1 billion. An unnamed source informed Wired that DeepSeek likely used around 50,000 Nvidia chips.

Despite limited disclosures, DeepSeek's reported costs highlight an accounting strategy designed to showcase efficiency. The company based its figures on rental-equivalent pricing, omitting investments in infrastructure. Reports indicate DeepSeek purchased 10,000 Nvidia A100 chips (pre-2023 U.S. export restrictions) and maintains a cluster of 50,000 H800s—modified for the Chinese market. Even without undisclosed assets, these purchases alone exceed $130 million.

Scaling vs. Optimization: The Future of AI

DeepSeek's approach underscores a key AI development question: Should the future focus on scaling or optimization?

China, facing U.S. semiconductor restrictions, has leveraged necessity-driven innovation to accelerate development. In contrast, the U.S. AI sector, dominated by Big Tech, follows a brute-force scaling strategy, investing in larger infrastructure and cutting-edge GPUs rather than optimizing efficiency. Startups like OpenAI, once disruptors, have matured into corporate giants, potentially vulnerable to nimbler challengers.

DeepSeek's disruption extends beyond China—it challenges Silicon Valley's economic model. The launch of DeepSeek-V2 in mid-2024 triggered a price war among Chinese tech giants, including ByteDance, Alibaba, Baidu, and Tencent, as well as AI startups like Zhipu AI. Unlike Huawei's government-backed semiconductor initiatives, DeepSeek appears to be a market-driven enterprise.

U.S. Response & Policy Implications

While DeepSeek's advancements rattled markets, the U.S. political response remained measured. President Trump called it a "wake-up call" for American industry, emphasizing the benefits of cost-efficient AI development. Shortly after revoking Biden's Executive Order 14110 on AI governance, the administration announced a $500 billion Stargate AI infrastructure project with OpenAI, Oracle, and SoftBank.

This raises pressing policy questions: Should the U.S. double down on export controls, or reconsider restrictions to allow Nvidia and other American firms to profit? DeepSeek's success demonstrates that AI development can continue despite chip limitations. Restrictive policies may delay progress but also incentivize Chinese innovation.

Export controls are inherently reactive. DeepSeek trained on Nvidia's H800s—chips specifically designed to comply with 2022 regulations. When additional restrictions closed that loophole, Nvidia introduced the H20, which, while weaker for training, remains viable for inference tasks. As AI development advances, policymakers must reassess whether restricting China's access to AI hardware strengthens U.S. leadership or merely accelerates alternative innovation paths.

The Growing AI Divide and DeepSeek's Controversy

Despite its efficiency gains, DeepSeek acknowledges a fourfold compute disadvantage compared to U.S. firms, largely due to export controls. As ChinaTalk reports, these restrictions remain the primary barrier for DeepSeek's progress, and they continue to widen the AI compute gap between the U.S. and China. To maintain this lead, the U.S. must reinforce, rather than weaken, its export controls.

The Trump administration is reportedly considering further restrictions on Nvidia chip exports to China, including a potential ban on the H20 chips—a scaled-down version for the Chinese market. However, Bloomberg sources suggest a decision may be delayed, given that Commerce Secretary nominee Howard Lutnick has yet to be confirmed, and the Department of Commerce is still in the early stages of staffing. Meanwhile, China may use this window to stockpile as many H20 chips as possible.

On the other hand, concerns are growing over Trump's proposed tariffs on Taiwanese chip imports. Taiwan's exports to the U.S. surged 46% last year to $111.3 billion, with AI servers and semiconductor components accounting for $67.9 billion—an 81% increase. This shift reflects Taiwan's direct exports replacing what was previously routed through China. Speaking at the House Republican Issues Convention, Trump criticized companies moving operations to Taiwan and threatened tariffs of up to 100% on foreign-produced semiconductors and pharmaceuticals to encourage domestic production. If enacted, these tariffs would significantly impact U.S. companies like AMD, Apple, Nvidia, and Qualcomm, which rely on Taiwan's TSMC. The added costs would inevitably trickle down to consumers, potentially damaging U.S. AI competitiveness at a critical moment.

Repatriating semiconductor manufacturing to the U.S. is a long-term goal requiring strategic policy support. Excessive tariffs, however, could cause immediate inflation and disrupt the industry. Some speculate Trump's rhetoric is a negotiating tactic aimed at securing concessions. Taiwan's Premier Cho Jung-tai has already responded, stating that Taiwan will consider cooperative plans to address these concerns.

DeepSeek's Data Risks and Security Concerns

DeepSeek's meteoric rise—propelling its app to the top of Apple's U.S. App Store—has sparked concerns about data security and censorship. Strategy Risks CEO Isaac Stone Fish likened its propaganda to making TikTok seem like a "Pentagon press conference." Unlike TikTok, DeepSeek explicitly states in its privacy policy that user data is stored on servers in China and governed by Chinese law.

The AI platform collects a wide range of user data, including text inputs, chat history, keystroke tracking, and uploaded files. Cybersecurity firm Wiz Research recently discovered an exposed DeepSeek database containing over a million lines of sensitive chat logs, which the company quickly secured after notification.

DeepSeek's censorship practices also mirror those of other Chinese platforms. Reports indicate it avoids politically sensitive topics, aligning with China's regulatory framework for AI services. AI security firm Promptfoo found its censorship methods to be "applied by brute force" and easy to detect, raising concerns about user data being used for future AI training.

Beyond DeepSeek's direct use in China, its models are now integrated into AI platforms worldwide, including Perplexity AI and Microsoft's Azure AI Foundry. While Perplexity claims its DeepSeek models operate independently on U.S. and EU servers, cybersecurity firm Ironscales warns that without rigorous code audits, hidden telemetry could still transmit data back to China. Additionally, questions remain about whether DeepSeek's censorship mechanisms persist in locally deployed versions.

For casual users, DeepSeek's security risks are particularly alarming. Studies indicate it is easier to bypass DeepSeek's safeguards compared to U.S. AI models, enabling it to generate phishing emails and malicious code. Enkrypt AI found that DeepSeek-R1 is four times more likely than OpenAI's models to generate malware. NewsGuard further reported that DeepSeek chatbot responses promoted foreign disinformation 35% of the time and reflected the Chinese government's perspective in 60% of cases. These concerns have led the U.S. House of Representatives to prohibit DeepSeek for official use.

While Trump previously downplayed TikTok's security risks, it remains unclear whether he will take a similarly lenient stance on DeepSeek. Meanwhile, European regulators have acted swiftly, launching GDPR investigations into DeepSeek's data practices. Italy removed the DeepSeek app from Apple and Google stores, and Ireland has begun its own inquiry into the company's data handling.

Allegations of Intellectual Property Theft

AI experts have long suspected that DeepSeek engaged in "knowledge distillation," a process where a smaller AI model is trained using outputs from a more advanced model. OpenAI, which explicitly prohibits competitors from using its outputs for model training, confirmed to the Financial Times that it had found "some evidence" of distillation, potentially linked to DeepSeek.

Microsoft security researchers detected large-scale data exfiltration via OpenAI's API last fall, later suspecting DeepSeek as the source. Some DeepSeek users also reported receiving responses that identified the model as "Microsoft Copilot" or "built on OpenAI's GPT-4 architecture," suggesting possible training data leakage.

The U.S. government has taken notice. White House AI and crypto czar David Sacks stated in a Fox interview that there was "substantial evidence" of DeepSeek distilling OpenAI's models. He predicted that U.S. AI firms would soon implement stricter safeguards against such practices.

DeepSeek's founder, Liang Wenfeng, has positioned the company as a symbol of Chinese innovation, claiming it does not merely copy Western models. However, the Chinese government has seized on the controversy to push a nationalist narrative, framing Western IP protection as an excuse to suppress China's tech rise. Meanwhile, OpenAI itself faces scrutiny over its training data, with ongoing lawsuits accusing it of using copyrighted content. The debate over AI ethics and intellectual property is far from settled.

Lessons from the DeepSeek Shock

Despite its setbacks, DeepSeek has demonstrated that China is closing the AI gap with the U.S. David Sacks has acknowledged that DeepSeek-R1 is nearly on par with OpenAI's o1 model, trailing by only three to six months. However, upcoming U.S. advancements, including OpenAI's anticipated o3 model, may further widen the lead.

The DeepSeek episode serves as a wake-up call for the U.S. AI industry to fortify its intellectual property protections, enhance cybersecurity measures, and enforce stricter regulations on data training. While China continues to advance, U.S. export controls remain a crucial tool in shaping the global AI race.

2.4 The Speed and Scale of AI's Impact on Industries

The rapid adoption of AI across industries is fundamentally altering the pace of business and economic development. While past technological revolutions unfolded over several decades, the speed at which AI is being integrated into everyday operations is unprecedented. This is due, in part, to the synergy between AI and other advanced technologies such as big data, cloud computing, and the Internet of Things (IoT). AI can analyze vast amounts of data generated by these technologies in real time, allowing industries to make faster, more informed decisions. This immediate feedback loop has significantly accelerated the speed at which industries can innovate and adapt to market demands.

In manufacturing, AI-driven robotics enhances production capabilities by improving precision and reducing error rates. Factories are now able to operate with minimal human intervention, resulting in faster production cycles and lower operational costs. AI-powered predictive maintenance systems are also being used to anticipate equipment failures, reducing downtime and increasing efficiency. These advancements are helping manufacturers achieve economies of scale faster than ever before, while also reducing the cost of goods for consumers.

The healthcare industry is similarly experiencing rapid transformation. AI is enabling faster and more accurate diagnoses, improving patient outcomes while reducing the workload for healthcare professionals. AI algorithms can analyze medical images with remarkable accuracy, identify patterns that may elude human clinicians, and predict patient responses to treatments based on their unique genetic makeup. This ability to provide personalized care at scale is revolutionizing healthcare delivery and has the potential to significantly lower costs while improving access to quality care.

In the financial sector, AI is automating processes such as loan approvals, fraud detection, and investment management. Algorithmic trading platforms, powered by AI, can analyze market data and execute trades in fractions of a second, far outpacing human traders. This speed gives financial institutions a competitive edge in the global marketplace, allowing them to capitalize on opportunities that were previously inaccessible. Furthermore, AI's ability to analyze vast datasets means that banks and financial institutions can offer more personalized financial services, such as tailored investment portfolios and credit products, to individual customers.

The scale of AI's impact is perhaps most evident in the retail sector. AI-powered recommendation engines, inventory management systems, and chatbots are reshaping the way retailers interact with customers. These systems not only streamline operations but also enhance the customer experience by offering personalized product suggestions and real-time customer support.

As AI continues to evolve, its ability to anticipate consumer needs and trends will likely become even more sophisticated, driving further changes in the retail landscape.

The scale of AI's impact is not limited to individual sectors—it is transforming the broader economy. As AI systems become more ubiquitous, they are reshaping labor markets and changing the nature of work itself. While AI offers tremendous opportunities for productivity gains and economic growth, it also poses significant challenges for workers who may find their skills rendered obsolete. This dynamic will require policymakers, businesses, and educational institutions to work together to ensure that the benefits of AI are widely shared and that workers are prepared for the jobs of the future.

In conclusion, the Fourth Industrial Revolution, driven by AI, is unlike any previous technological shift in terms of its speed, scale, and impact on both industries and the global economy. As AI continues to evolve, it is poised to redefine the way we work, live, and interact with the world around us. Understanding and preparing for this transformation will be essential to ensure that the benefits of AI are realized in a way that is inclusive, equitable, and sustainable.

Chapter 3: AGI vs Human Labor

3.1 A Comparison of Human Cognitive Abilities and AGI's Projected Abilities

As Artificial General Intelligence (AGI) continues to develop, one of the most pressing questions is how its abilities will compare to human cognition. Human intelligence is characterized by a combination of several unique cognitive features: creativity, emotional intelligence, intuition, and the ability to adapt to new and unpredictable environments. AGI, by contrast, would be designed to replicate these capabilities, potentially even surpassing them in terms of speed, accuracy, and breadth of knowledge.

One of the most significant differences between AGI and human intelligence is the capacity for learning. Humans have an innate ability to learn from experience, mistakes, and their environment, forming abstract concepts, and applying this knowledge flexibly across different domains. AGI, once fully developed, would likely be able to learn at a rate far exceeding that of any human. With access to vast amounts of data and unparalleled processing power, AGI could draw from countless sources of information, making connections and deriving insights that are beyond the reach of human cognition. However, while AGI might outperform humans in processing data and pattern recognition, human cognition remains deeply tied to subjective experiences and emotional depth, which gives rise to empathy, creativity, and ethical reasoning. These are areas where AGI might still struggle to replicate the full complexity of human thought.

AGI's projected abilities also suggest that it will be able to handle tasks that require immense cognitive effort, such as making complex calculations, solving intricate problems across disciplines, and managing large-scale operations that involve multiple variables and outcomes. However, while AGI may excel at logical reasoning, pattern recognition, and optimization tasks, it is uncertain whether it will be able to match humans in areas like emotional intelligence, empathy, and ethical decision-making. These aspects of cognition, which are often central to human relationships, leadership, and moral reasoning, might remain exclusive to humans for the foreseeable future.

Additionally, AGI would have the ability to continuously upgrade and improve itself, which is something humans cannot do at the same pace. This self-improving ability means that AGI could eventually surpass human intelligence in most areas, raising concerns about its potential to dominate industries that rely on cognitive skills traditionally associated with human workers. The question then becomes not just whether AGI will be able to replicate human cognition, but how far it will go beyond it.

3.2 Tasks that will remain exclusive to Humans vs tasks that AGI will outperform

Despite AGI's remarkable potential, there are certain tasks that may remain the exclusive domain of humans, at least in the short-to-medium term. These tasks typically require deep emotional engagement, empathy, moral reasoning, or the use of nuanced cultural and social understanding. Professions such as caregiving, counseling, education, and roles that require human interaction at a personal level may still benefit from the irreplaceable human touch. For example, while AGI might be able to provide medical diagnoses with high accuracy, it may not be capable of delivering difficult news with the empathy and compassion required in such situations. Similarly, in creative fields like writing, music, and art, where personal expression and cultural resonance are key, humans may continue to lead, even as AGI aids in the production process.

However, AGI will likely outperform humans in tasks that require repetitive cognitive processing, such as data analysis, and high-level decision-making from large datasets. Jobs in sectors such as finance, law, logistics, and healthcare could see AGI surpass human workers in areas like contract analysis, fraud detection, supply chain management, and even medical diagnosis. In these roles, AGI's ability to process and analyze vast amounts of information quickly and efficiently will give it a significant advantage. For instance, in legal settings, AGI could analyze case histories, legal documents, and precedents far more effectively than any human lawyer, providing more accurate predictions of case outcomes and legal strategies. Similarly, in healthcare, AGI could analyze patient data, medical histories, and cutting-edge research to provide more personalized and effective treatment plans than a human physician alone.

In fields that require complex problem-solving and high levels of coordination, such as engineering and logistics, AGI's capacity to manage multiple variables and scenarios simultaneously will make it superior to humans in many tasks. For example, in supply chain management, AGI could optimize routes, forecast demand, and ensure that materials are delivered in the most efficient way possible, with minimal human oversight. In scientific research, AGI could rapidly conduct simulations, design experiments, and analyze results, accelerating the pace of discovery in fields ranging from biology to physics.

Moreover, AGI is likely to outperform humans in any task where speed, precision, and consistency are paramount. In industries such as manufacturing, where repetitive tasks dominate, AGI could oversee and automate entire production processes, ensuring greater efficiency and fewer errors. While traditional robots and Narrow AI are already making strides in these areas, AGI would bring a level of adaptability and decision-making capability that surpasses existing automation technologies. For example, AGI could dynamically adjust production lines based on real-time data, quickly responding to changes in demand or supply chain disruptions.

3.3 Potential Sectors at Risk for Displacement and Sectors That May Benefit

As AGI continues to develop, certain sectors are at a higher risk of job displacement than others. Industries that rely heavily on routine tasks, data analysis, and decision-making based on large datasets will likely see the most significant impacts. The finance sector, for instance, is at high risk of displacement as AGI could automate tasks such as trading, risk assessment, loan approvals, and even financial advising. Financial analysts, traders, and auditors could see their roles diminished or eliminated as AGI takes over these cognitive tasks more efficiently and accurately.

Figure 3.1: Office workers laid-off due to implementation of AI-agents

Similarly, the legal profession may experience significant disruption. While legal work has traditionally required human expertise in interpreting laws and precedents, AGI could be used to automate many of the more repetitive and time-consuming tasks that lawyers and paralegals perform. Contract drafting, case analysis, and legal research could be largely managed by AGI systems, reducing the demand for human labor in these areas. Some lawyers might still be required for courtroom advocacy or high-level negotiations, but the profession as a whole could undergo significant downsizing.

Healthcare is another sector that stands to see major transformations due to AGI. While doctors and nurses will still be needed for patient care and human interaction, AGI could take over many diagnostic and administrative tasks. AGI's ability to analyze medical records, lab results, and scientific research could lead to more accurate and personalized treatments, reducing the need for large teams of specialists. Radiologists, for instance, are at particular risk as AGI systems could eventually surpass human capabilities in reading and interpreting medical images. Similarly, pharmaceutical research could be revolutionized by AGI, leading to faster drug discovery and development processes.

However, not all sectors will experience negative impacts from the rise of AGI. Some industries may actually benefit from AGI's capabilities, particularly those that require advanced problem-solving and innovation. For instance, the technology sector is likely to thrive as AGI becomes a key tool for software development, cybersecurity, and AI-enhanced product design. AGI could enable faster and more efficient coding, as well as the creation of more sophisticated and secure digital systems. In research and development, AGI could drive innovation in fields such as biotechnology, renewable energy, and material science, pushing the boundaries of what is possible in terms of new discoveries and technological breakthroughs.

Education is another sector that could benefit from AGI, though it may require a rethinking of traditional teaching models. AGI could be used to create personalized learning experiences, adapting curricula and teaching methods to the unique needs of each student. Teachers, rather than being replaced, could focus more on fostering critical thinking, creativity, and social skills, while AGI handles more of the administrative and instructional tasks.

The creative industries could also see gains from AGI, particularly in areas like media production, advertising, and game design. AGI could be used to automate many aspects of content creation, such as generating scripts, designing characters, or editing videos, freeing up human creators to focus on more high-level creative decisions. AGI could also be used to analyze audience data, providing insights that allow creators to tailor their work to specific markets more effectively.

Conclusion

The rise of AGI presents a complex and multifaceted challenge for the global job market. While AGI's potential to outperform humans in certain cognitive tasks is undeniable, there remain areas where human intelligence, empathy, and creativity will continue to hold value. The key question is how industries and economies will adapt to the changes brought by AGI. Sectors that rely heavily on routine, data-driven tasks are at the greatest risk of displacement, while industries that require innovation, creativity, and human interaction may not only survive but also thrive in the AGI era.

The future of work in the age of AGI will depend on how effectively societies manage the transition. Reskilling and upskilling will be crucial to ensuring that workers can move into new roles that leverage human abilities that AGI cannot replicate. Policymakers, businesses, and educators will need to collaborate to create a future where AGI complements human labor rather than replacing it entirely. As AGI continues to evolve, the challenge will be to harness its power for the benefit of all, while mitigating its potential to disrupt lives and livelihoods.

PART 2: THE FUTURE OF JOBS IN THE U.S.

Chapter 4: Key Industries Transformed by AGI

4.1 Manufacturing and Automation

The manufacturing industry has long been at the forefront of technological advancements, from mechanization during the First Industrial Revolution to the rise of robotics and automation in the late 20th century. The introduction of Artificial General Intelligence (AGI) will mark a new chapter in this evolution, transforming manufacturing processes in ways that are both profound and wide-ranging. While Narrow AI and robotics have already made significant strides in automating repetitive tasks and optimizing production lines, AGI will enable far more sophisticated automation, bringing human-level problem-solving, decision-making, and adaptability to manufacturing systems.

One of the key ways AGI will transform manufacturing is through "smart" production systems. These systems will use AGI to monitor and manage all aspects of the production process, from raw material acquisition to final product assembly, with minimal human intervention. AGI will be able to make real-time adjustments to production lines based on changing market conditions, supply chain disruptions, or customer preferences. For instance, if there is a shortage of a particular component, AGI systems could dynamically adjust production schedules or find alternative suppliers, ensuring that operations continue smoothly without delays. This level of flexibility and responsiveness will vastly improve efficiency and reduce downtime.

In addition to optimizing current production processes, AGI will play a critical role in product design and innovation. By analyzing vast amounts of data on consumer preferences, market trends, and material properties, AGI can help manufacturers design products that are more in tune with customer demands. Moreover, AGI can run complex simulations to test new designs and materials in virtual environments, reducing the need for costly physical prototypes and speeding up the time-to-market for new products. This will lead to more rapid cycles of innovation, allowing manufacturers to stay competitive in a fast-evolving global economy.

Figure 4.1: A large cluster of computers in a data center

AGI will also have a significant impact on workforce dynamics in the manufacturing sector. While robots and AI systems have already displaced many manual labor roles, AGI's ability to perform complex cognitive tasks will result in the displacement of even more high-skilled jobs, such as those held by engineers, managers, and planners. However, new opportunities will also arise as AGI creates demand for workers who can manage, maintain, and improve AGI-driven systems. Reskilling and upskilling will be essential to help the manufacturing workforce transition to new roles that require more strategic thinking, creativity, and oversight of AGI systems.

4.2 Healthcare and Medical Professions

The healthcare industry is poised to undergo significant transformation as AGI becomes a critical tool for enhancing patient care, improving diagnostics, and optimizing treatment plans. AGI's ability to process and analyze vast amounts of medical data will revolutionize how healthcare professionals diagnose diseases, manage treatment plans, and deliver personalized care. Unlike Narrow AI, which is currently used in specific applications such as radiology or predictive analytics, AGI will be capable of synthesizing data from multiple sources, providing a more holistic approach to patient care.

In diagnostics, AGI will be able to analyze medical records, laboratory results, imaging data, and even genetic information to detect patterns and make accurate diagnoses. AGI's ability to analyze complex data sets far exceeds that of any human doctor, allowing it to identify rare diseases or subtle indicators that might otherwise go unnoticed. This could lead to earlier detection of conditions such as cancer, cardiovascular diseases, and neurodegenerative disorders, where early intervention is critical to patient outcomes. Additionally, AGI systems could continuously monitor patient data in real-time, providing immediate feedback to healthcare providers if a patient's condition changes.

Beyond diagnostics, AGI will play a pivotal role in personalized medicine. By analyzing individual patient data alongside the latest research, AGI can recommend customized treatment plans tailored to each patient's genetic makeup, lifestyle, and medical history. This will allow for more effective treatments, fewer side effects, and faster recovery times. AGI will also contribute to drug discovery and development, helping researchers identify potential new treatments by analyzing vast datasets of biological information, clinical trial results, and chemical compounds. This could significantly reduce the time and cost associated with bringing new drugs to market.

However, the integration of AGI into healthcare raises significant ethical and regulatory questions. As AGI begins to make critical decisions about patient care, who will be held accountable for mistakes or adverse outcomes? Moreover, while AGI can process data and provide recommendations, the importance of human empathy, trust, and communication in healthcare cannot be overstated. Patients may still prefer to interact with human doctors for diagnoses and treatments, emphasizing the need for a balanced approach where AGI supports healthcare professionals without completely replacing them.

4.3 Finance and Banking

The finance and banking industry is another sector that will experience widespread transformation due to AGI. Financial institutions have already embraced automation and Narrow AI to enhance risk assessment, fraud detection, and customer service. However, AGI's broader cognitive capabilities will take these advancements to the next level, enabling more sophisticated decision-making and predictive analysis in areas such as investment strategies, credit risk management, and regulatory compliance.

In investment and asset management, AGI will be able to analyze global financial markets in real-time, identify emerging trends, and make highly informed investment decisions with precision. While current AI-driven trading systems rely on specific algorithms designed to recognize patterns in market data, AGI will be able to understand broader economic conditions, geopolitical factors, and even social and environmental trends to create more accurate forecasts and portfolio recommendations. AGI will be able to adapt its strategies on the fly, reacting to changes in the market faster than any human trader or current AI system.

AGI will also revolutionize the banking sector's approach to risk management. Traditionally, banks have relied on historical data and human judgment to assess credit risk, identify potential defaults, and manage loans. With AGI, banks will be able to consider a far greater array of data points, including non-traditional indicators such as social media behavior or online purchasing patterns, to create more comprehensive and accurate risk profiles. This could lead to more inclusive lending practices, opening up financial opportunities to individuals and businesses who might have been overlooked by traditional risk assessment models.

In addition to these advancements, AGI will improve cybersecurity and fraud detection within the financial sector. Cyberattacks and financial fraud have become increasingly sophisticated, and AGI systems will be able to detect and respond to these threats more effectively than human teams or current AI technologies. AGI's ability to monitor and analyze transactions in real-time will help financial institutions identify suspicious behavior and prevent fraudulent activities before they result in significant losses.

However, as with other industries, the rise of AGI in finance and banking will also lead to job displacement. Many roles traditionally performed by financial analysts, traders, and compliance officers may be automated by AGI systems. At the same time, new opportunities will arise in areas such as data analysis, system oversight, and regulatory management, creating a demand for workers with expertise in managing AGI-driven financial systems.

4.4 Transportation and Logistics

Transportation and logistics is another industry that stands to be profoundly transformed by AGI. While autonomous vehicles and drones are already being developed and tested using Narrow AI, the advent of AGI will enable these systems to operate with a much higher degree of autonomy, flexibility, and intelligence. AGI systems will be able to navigate complex transportation networks, optimize delivery routes, and manage entire fleets of vehicles with little to no human intervention.

In logistics, AGI will enable real-time optimization of supply chains, ensuring that goods are delivered in the most efficient and cost-effective manner. By analyzing data from weather patterns, traffic conditions, and market demand, AGI systems can dynamically adjust delivery routes and schedules, minimizing delays and reducing fuel consumption. This will be particularly important in industries such as e-commerce, where timely delivery is a key factor in customer satisfaction.

Autonomous vehicles, powered by AGI, will revolutionize both personal and commercial transportation. AGI-driven vehicles will be able to make real-time decisions based on a vast array of data, allowing them to navigate safely and efficiently in complex environments. In commercial transportation, this will reduce the need for human drivers, leading to significant cost savings for companies and potentially reshaping the labor market for truck drivers, delivery personnel, and other transportation workers. However, the widespread adoption of autonomous vehicles will also raise ethical and regulatory challenges, particularly in terms of safety, liability, and the potential displacement of millions of workers.

4.5 Education and Training

AGI will also have a transformative impact on education and training, offering new opportunities for personalized learning, teacher support, and skills development. In traditional educational settings, AGI will be able to adapt curricula and teaching methods to the individual needs of each student, providing tailored learning experiences that maximize engagement and comprehension.

AGI systems will analyze student performance data to identify areas where students are struggling, recommend targeted interventions, and adjust the pace of instruction to suit the learner's progress.

For teachers, AGI will serve as a valuable tool for managing administrative tasks, grading assignments, and providing real-time feedback to students. By automating these routine responsibilities, teachers will have more time to focus on fostering creativity, critical thinking, and social-emotional learning, which are areas where human educators excel. Additionally, AGI could be used to create virtual teaching assistants, capable of answering student questions, guiding them through complex concepts, and providing additional support outside of the classroom.

In corporate training and skills development, AGI will enable more efficient and effective learning programs. AGI-powered systems will be able to assess an individual's current skill set and create personalized learning paths designed to help them acquire new skills relevant to their career goals. This will be particularly important in an economy where the pace of technological change is accelerating, and workers need to continuously update their skills to remain competitive in the job market.

While AGI presents significant opportunities for improving education and training outcomes, it also raises questions about equity and access. Will AGI-driven educational tools be available to all students, regardless of socioeconomic background? How can educators ensure that AGI is used ethically and inclusively? These are important considerations that will need to be addressed as AGI becomes more integrated into the educational landscape.

Figure 4.2: School children being taught lessons by an AI instructor

Chapter 5: Economic Displacement and Job Losses

5.1 Projections of Job Displacement due to AGI in various sectors

The advent of Artificial General Intelligence (AGI) is poised to create significant disruptions in the global job market, with widespread projections of job displacement across various sectors. While earlier technological revolutions displaced manual labor, AGI introduces the concept of cognitive automation, enabling machines to perform complex decision-making, problem-solving, and creative tasks traditionally reserved for humans. This development goes beyond what Narrow AI has achieved, as AGI will not be limited to predefined tasks but will have the ability to learn, adapt, and evolve, making its presence felt across a broader range of industries.

In manufacturing and automation, AGI is expected to replace workers who perform both low-skilled and high-skilled tasks. Unlike earlier technological advancements that predominantly affected manual labor, AGI will also displace roles such as quality control engineers, logistics managers, and even product designers. AGI's ability to adapt to dynamic production needs, make real-time decisions, and optimize processes will reduce the need for human oversight and intervention. Factories of the future could run almost entirely autonomously, with AGI monitoring supply chains, managing production lines, and even creating new product designs based on market data.

Healthcare is another sector that could see significant disruption. While the field is traditionally resistant to automation due to the complexity of human interaction and empathy required, AGI's potential to handle diagnostics, medical records analysis, treatment plans, and even patient monitoring raises the likelihood of job displacement.

Radiologists, diagnosticians, and even some roles in surgery could be supplemented or replaced by AGI systems that outperform humans in terms of speed and accuracy. However, jobs requiring interpersonal communication and emotional intelligence, such as nursing and mental health care, may be more resistant to displacement.

In the finance and banking industry, AGI will revolutionize trading, risk management, and customer service. Highly cognitive roles such as financial analysts, investment bankers, and compliance officers may be at risk as AGI systems become capable of making complex financial decisions and predicting market trends with greater precision.

Figure 5.1: AGI as a major disruption to various job sectors

AGI will also streamline customer service operations by providing personalized assistance through advanced chatbots and virtual advisors, reducing the need for human customer service representatives.

The transportation and logistics industry will experience significant disruption as AGI enables fully autonomous vehicles, drones, and supply chain management systems. Truck drivers, delivery personnel, and logistics coordinators will face substantial displacement as AGI-driven systems take over these roles. Furthermore, AGI's ability to optimize supply chain operations and dynamically reroute shipments will eliminate the need for human decision-makers in this sector.

Education, while more resilient to AGI's impact, may still experience job displacement, particularly in administrative and support roles. AGI will automate grading, student progress tracking, and even personalized tutoring. Teachers may find that their roles evolve to focus more on facilitating human interaction, creativity, and emotional intelligence, areas where AGI will struggle to replicate the human experience.

5.2 The Role of AGI in Automation Beyond Physical Labor: Cognitive Automation

The term “automation” has traditionally been associated with the mechanization of physical tasks—factory workers being replaced by machines, or logistics operations being managed by robotic systems. However, AGI introduces the concept of cognitive automation, which goes beyond the automation of physical labor to encompass tasks that require cognitive skills. Cognitive automation refers to AGI’s ability to perform tasks that involve complex thinking, decision-making, learning, and creativity—areas traditionally considered the exclusive domain of humans.

Cognitive automation will disrupt many white-collar jobs. For instance, AGI systems can rapidly analyze vast datasets, identify trends, and make predictions, which is a core part of roles such as data analysts, financial planners, and consultants. In legal professions, AGI can analyze case law, draft legal documents, and predict case outcomes more efficiently than human lawyers.

Similarly, in the medical field, AGI’s ability to diagnose diseases based on medical imaging or patient data will surpass the diagnostic capabilities of many healthcare professionals.

One key aspect of cognitive automation is AGI’s capacity for learning and adaptation. Unlike traditional software systems or Narrow AI, which perform only pre-defined tasks, AGI can learn from its environment, adapt to new information, and improve its decision-making over time. This means that AGI will not only replace repetitive cognitive tasks but also dynamic, high-level functions previously thought to be out of reach for machines.

Creative professions, such as design, marketing, and even writing, are not immune to AGI’s influence. With AGI’s ability to generate ideas, design products, and create content based on data-driven insights, professionals in these fields may find that their roles shift from active creators to curators or supervisors of AGI-generated work. The distinction between human and machine creativity will blur as AGI systems become capable of producing works that are indistinguishable from those made by humans.

However, cognitive automation will not lead to a total replacement of human labor. Instead, it will redefine the nature of work, with humans taking on roles that require emotional intelligence, ethical judgment, and interpersonal communication. For example, while AGI may outperform humans in analyzing financial markets or diagnosing diseases, it will struggle with tasks that require empathy, cultural understanding, and ethical decision-making. Cognitive automation will thus create opportunities for humans to focus on more strategic, relational, and creative aspects of work, while AGI handles the routine, data-driven tasks.

5.3 Comparison of Rural vs Urban Job Impacts

The impact of AGI on jobs will not be uniform across geographic regions. Rural and urban areas will experience the effects of AGI-driven automation differently, based on the types of industries that dominate these regions and the availability of infrastructure to support AGI integration.

In urban areas, where economies are typically more diverse and reliant on sectors such as finance, technology, and healthcare, AGI will lead to significant job displacement in white-collar and high-skill jobs. Many urban professionals in roles such as financial analysts, legal advisors, medical diagnosticians, and engineers will see their jobs transformed or replaced by AGI systems. However, urban areas are also likely to benefit from new job opportunities in AGI-related fields such as AI development, cybersecurity, and data science. As urban centers are often hubs of technological innovation, they will be better positioned to adapt to the disruptions caused by AGI and to capitalize on the economic benefits of this new technology.

Conversely, rural areas, which tend to rely more heavily on agriculture, manufacturing, and transportation, may face more severe economic disruption. Many of these industries are prime candidates for AGI-driven automation, particularly in manufacturing and logistics.

The widespread adoption of AGI in these sectors could lead to significant job losses, as factory workers, truck drivers, and other blue-collar workers are displaced by autonomous systems. The lack of infrastructure and investment in AGI technology in rural areas may also limit the ability of these regions to create new opportunities in AGI-related fields, exacerbating economic inequality between urban and rural regions.

In the agriculture sector, AGI-driven systems could revolutionize farming through precision agriculture, autonomous tractors, and intelligent supply chain management. While these advancements will increase efficiency and reduce costs, they will also lead to the displacement of farm laborers and agricultural workers who rely on these jobs for their livelihoods. However, rural areas that embrace AGI technology in agriculture may find new opportunities in managing and maintaining these systems, potentially creating high-skilled jobs that require expertise in AI, robotics, and data analytics.

Transportation and logistics, which are critical industries in both rural and urban areas, will also experience uneven impacts from AGI. In urban regions, autonomous delivery vehicles and AGI-driven supply chain management will reduce the need for human workers in delivery, warehousing, and logistics coordination. In rural areas, where transportation is often a key source of employment, the displacement of truck drivers and other transportation workers could have a more profound economic impact. AGI's ability to optimize long-distance logistics and manage transportation networks will lead to significant job losses in rural communities that depend on these industries.

Figure 5.2: AGI affecting transportation and logistics, within critical industries

To mitigate the effects of AGI-driven displacement, governments, businesses, and educational institutions will need to invest in retraining programs and reskilling initiatives that prepare workers for the new roles created by AGI technology. In both rural and urban areas, the focus should be on developing skills in areas such as AI system management, cybersecurity, data analytics, and human-centered professions that require emotional intelligence and ethical decision-making. Additionally, policies aimed at promoting equitable access to AGI-related opportunities, particularly in rural areas, will be essential to ensuring that the benefits of AGI are shared broadly across society.

Conclusion

As AGI continues to develop, its impact on the economy will be far-reaching, with significant job displacement projected across various sectors. Cognitive automation will redefine the nature of work, with AGI taking over tasks that require not only physical labor but also complex thinking and decision-making. While urban areas may benefit from new job opportunities in AGI-related fields, rural areas may face more profound economic disruption as key industries are automated. To navigate this transition, it is essential to invest in reskilling programs and ensure that all regions, both rural and urban, are prepared to benefit from the AGI-driven economy.

Chapter 6: New Job Creation and Emerging Industries

6.1 Sectors Where AGI Will Create New Opportunities

While concerns over job displacement due to Artificial General Intelligence (AGI) are widespread, AGI will also open up new opportunities and create entirely new sectors within the global economy. As AGI becomes more integrated into various industries, there will be a growing demand for new types of expertise, particularly in areas where humans and AGI systems collaborate, innovate, and manage AGI technology. These emerging sectors will likely form the backbone of future economies, and understanding where these new opportunities lie will be crucial for preparing workers and industries to thrive in an AI-driven world.

One major sector where AGI will create opportunities is in AI research and development. As AGI systems advance, there will be a continuous need for experts to push the boundaries of AGI's capabilities, design more efficient algorithms, and improve the systems' safety and reliability. This will lead to a surge in demand for AI researchers, computer scientists, and engineers specializing in machine learning, natural language processing, and neural networks. Furthermore, the interdisciplinary nature of AGI will require collaboration with specialists in neuroscience, cognitive science, and robotics to ensure that AGI systems can integrate effectively with human environments and behaviors.

Another sector poised for growth is cybersecurity. As AGI takes on more decision-making roles in critical systems, including healthcare, finance, and national defense, the need for securing these systems from cyberattacks will become paramount. Experts in cybersecurity will be tasked with developing advanced protection mechanisms to safeguard AGI-driven infrastructure, creating a demand for specialized roles in AI security, data encryption, and ethical hacking. New companies may emerge that focus exclusively on providing security solutions for AGI applications, further expanding job opportunities within this sector.

Figure 6.1: Tech job fair

Healthcare is also an industry where AGI will open new avenues for innovation. While AGI will take over routine diagnostic and administrative tasks, new roles will emerge for healthcare professionals working alongside AGI to provide personalized care. This may include roles like AI-assisted health coaches, who use AGI data analysis to craft personalized health plans for patients, or AGI-guided surgeons, who collaborate with AGI systems to ensure precise, error-free procedures. The rise of telemedicine, driven by AGI-enabled diagnostics and patient monitoring, will create opportunities for medical professionals to serve larger patient populations remotely, leveraging AGI to enhance patient care across vast distances.

In addition, AGI will play a significant role in sustainability and environmental sectors. As industries work to reduce carbon emissions and adapt to changing environmental regulations, AGI will be crucial in optimizing energy usage, managing renewable resources, and developing sustainable technologies. New jobs will be created in fields like AI-driven environmental management, where AGI is used to monitor ecosystems, track climate data, and suggest interventions to mitigate environmental damage. Similarly, AI-powered agriculture will require specialists who can manage AGI systems for precision farming, optimizing crop yields while minimizing resource consumption.

6.2 Jobs That Will Require Human-AI Collaboration

One of the key transformations AGI will bring to the job market is the rise of jobs that require human-AI collaboration. While AGI will excel in data analysis, pattern recognition, and automating complex tasks, there are many areas where human creativity, emotional intelligence, and ethical decision-making will still be essential. The jobs of the future will likely involve working alongside AGI to enhance productivity and decision-making processes rather than fully replacing human labor.

In sectors like creative industries, including marketing, advertising, and content creation—AGI will assist in generating ideas, analyzing market trends, and optimizing campaigns. However, humans will still be needed to provide the cultural and emotional insights that are essential for creating content that resonates with audiences. Human-AI collaboration in creative design will involve individuals working closely with AGI to explore new artistic directions, enhance storytelling, and tailor messaging to specific demographics. For example, while AGI may generate multiple design prototypes or advertising strategies, humans will make the final decisions about which ideas are most effective in connecting with consumers.

In education, teachers will collaborate with AGI systems to deliver personalized learning experiences. AGI will handle the data-driven aspects of education, such as analyzing student performance, tailoring lesson plans, and identifying areas where students need additional support. However, teachers will continue to play a vital role in providing emotional support, fostering critical thinking, and encouraging creativity in students. AI-assisted educators will work with AGI to enhance their teaching methods, allowing for more individualized attention while focusing on developing students' emotional and social intelligence.

In healthcare, AI-assisted physicians and surgeons will use AGI to improve diagnostic accuracy and perform surgeries with greater precision. AGI systems will analyze vast amounts of patient data, suggest treatment plans, and predict health outcomes, but doctors will still be responsible for making the final decisions about patient care. Human compassion, ethical judgment, and the ability to communicate complex medical information in an empathetic manner will remain essential aspects of healthcare, ensuring that human-AI collaboration enhances, rather than replaces, the patient-doctor relationship.

FIGURE 6.2: AI research and development

6.3 Growth of AI Maintenance, Ethics, and Regulation-Related

As AGI systems become integral to a wide range of industries, the need for AI maintenance and support roles will grow exponentially. These jobs will focus on ensuring that AGI systems are operating efficiently, safely, and ethically. For example, AI system managers will oversee the day-to-day operations of AGI systems, monitor their performance, and troubleshoot any issues that arise. As AGI systems are complex and continually evolving, these roles will require individuals with advanced technical knowledge and the ability to keep up with rapid advancements in AI technology.

In addition to technical support, there will be a growing demand for AI ethicists and professionals involved in AI governance. The ethical implications of AGI, particularly regarding its decision-making autonomy, bias, and societal impact, will require careful regulation. Governments, companies, and international organizations will need experts who can establish ethical frameworks for AGI, ensuring that its deployment aligns with human values. AI ethics officers will work within organizations to monitor AGI's actions, prevent unethical behavior, and ensure compliance with both legal and moral standards.

Regulation-related professions will also expand as governments worldwide grapple with the legal and societal implications of AGI. Policymakers and legal professionals specializing in AI regulation will need to develop frameworks for governing AGI's use in everything from healthcare and finance to autonomous weapons and data privacy. Regulatory compliance officers will ensure that companies using AGI adhere to these laws, while AI policy advisors will play a crucial role in shaping public policy around AGI, advising governments on the potential risks and benefits of its adoption.

6.4 Entrepreneurial Opportunities in an AI-Driven Economy

The rise of AGI will bring about an explosion of entrepreneurial opportunities. As industries adapt to AGI, startups and new ventures will emerge to take advantage of the unique capabilities AGI offers. Entrepreneurs will develop AGI-driven products and services that solve problems in ways previously unimaginable, ranging from AI-powered personal assistants that can manage an individual's entire digital life to AGI-based medical solutions that provide affordable healthcare to underserved populations.

In a 2025 interview with GreylockVC, OpenAI's CEO Sam Altman discussed the future landscape of AI startups. He predicted that only a few foundational large models will dominate the AI space, serving as the core infrastructure upon which developers will build. For example, a company might develop a large language model along with an API (Application Programming Interface), enabling software engineers to integrate it into their applications.

Altman emphasized the significance of a middle layer in this ecosystem, where numerous startups will leverage these large models, refining them far beyond traditional fine-tuning.

He further explained that extensive access to these models will allow companies to develop specialized applications tailored to fields such as medicine, human-computer interaction, or even AI companions. This middle layer, where companies customize and optimize existing models for specific use cases, will generate substantial long-term value.

One area ripe for entrepreneurship is customized AI solutions for small and medium-sized businesses. As AGI systems become more affordable, smaller companies will need tailored AGI systems that meet their specific needs. Entrepreneurs who can create scalable AGI systems for niche industries, such as agriculture, construction, or hospitality, will find a wealth of opportunities.

Additionally, AI-based platforms for education, entertainment, and social interaction will emerge, offering personalized experiences driven by AGI's ability to learn and adapt to user preferences.

6.5 SaaS vs AaaS Software applications and services

The SaaS (Software as a Service) market and the Agentic Agent Systems (AAAS - Agent as a Service) market represent two distinct but converging fields. Here are some key differences between them:

1. **Nature of Services:**

    SaaS offers cloud-based software applications that users access over the internet. These tools are typically predefined, focused on specific tasks (e.g., CRM, accounting, collaboration), and provide a user interface for interaction. The user is the main operator, leveraging the software to complete tasks. (This is most common and traditional ecosystem in today's markets).

    AssA refers to the provision of intelligent, autonomous AI agents that can perform complex tasks on behalf of the user. These agents learn from data, make decisions, and interact with other systems with minimal human input. AaaS agents are designed to adapt, automate, and improve their efficiency over time without requiring manual intervention.

2. Task Handling:

SaaS tools are still largely task-specific. Users interact with them directly to perform their jobs (e.g., using a SaaS CRM tool to manage leads or a file storage system to store documents).

AssA systems, however, take automation to the next level. They act as intelligent assistants that not only help with tasks but can handle entire processes, make predictions, and adjust strategies autonomously.

3. User Interaction:

SaaS requires users to understand and manage the system. While these tools are becoming more intuitive, they still demand a certain level of user input for execution.

AssA interacts with users in a more passive and supportive way. They don't just respond to commands but also anticipate needs, analyze data, and recommend actions. Users might only need to provide initial parameters or goals, and the AI agent takes over.

4. Customization and Flexibility:

SaaS tools typically offer predefined functionalities and customization options, but the core structure remains static.

AssA, on the other hand, offers a high degree of flexibility. The agent can adapt and learn from each interaction, customizing its approach based on the environment, the tasks it performs, and user preferences.

Future Predictions:

AssA surpassing SaaS: It is predicted that the AaaS market will surpass the SaaS market due to several reasons:

1. **Automation and Efficiency**: AI agents will be able to automate complex tasks, making them more efficient than traditional SaaS tools.
2. **Smarter and Adaptive Systems:** As AI agents learn from the context and data, they will continuously improve and adapt, leading to more effective problem-solving and task completion.
3. **Reduction in Human Dependency:** Unlike SaaS tools that require constant user input, AI agents will reduce the need for human oversight and

intervention, making them a more attractive choice for businesses and individuals.

4. **Scalability:** AaaS can scale with the business by continuously learning and adjusting to new tasks, markets, or customer needs without additional development costs, whereas SaaS tools may require updates and manual customization to keep up with business changes.

In the near future, for every SaaS tool that exists, there could be a corresponding AI agent that automates, manages, and optimizes tasks in a way that SaaS tools currently cannot. As AI technology advances, the potential for AaaS to surpass SaaS becomes more viable, and businesses will likely prefer AI agents for their efficiency, adaptability, and potential to reduce operational costs.

Entrepreneurs will also find opportunities in AI-driven sustainability initiatives, creating AGI systems that help businesses and governments optimize energy use, reduce waste, and transition to renewable energy sources. In the field of transportation, AGI-driven logistics and autonomous vehicle startups will revolutionize how goods and people move, creating new markets and services. The sharing economy will be transformed by AGI, with platforms emerging that use AGI to optimize asset utilization, whether in housing, transportation, or other sectors.

AI-related education and training services will be a booming area for entrepreneurship. As workers across various sectors need to learn how to collaborate with AGI and use AGI systems effectively, there will be a high demand for training programs, online courses, and workshops that teach these skills. Entrepreneurs who can design engaging, effective learning experiences that help people transition to the AI-driven workforce will find a thriving market.

6.6 The Stargate Project

The Stargate Project is a monumental initiative launched in January 2025, aiming to establish the United States as a global leader in artificial intelligence (AI) infrastructure. With an investment of up to $500 billion over the next four years, the project seeks to construct advanced AI data centers and related facilities across the nation, thereby enhancing the country's technological capabilities.

A consortium of prominent stakeholders spearheads the Stargate Project. OpenAI, a leading AI research organization, brings its expertise in developing cutting-edge AI models. SoftBank Group Corp., a Japanese multinational conglomerate, contributes substantial financial backing and strategic oversight. Oracle Corporation, renowned for its enterprise software solutions, offers robust cloud computing infrastructure essential for the project's success. These collaborations underscore a unified effort to bolster AI infrastructure in the United States.

The mission of the Stargate Project encompasses several key objectives. Foremost is the development of state-of-the-art data centers, starting in Texas, to support the burgeoning demands of AI applications. This infrastructure is anticipated to create over 100,000 American jobs, thereby stimulating economic growth and technological innovation. Additionally, the project aims to maintain and enhance the United States' competitive edge in AI, particularly in the face of global advancements in the field.

Beyond economic and technological aspirations, the Stargate Project envisions significant societal benefits. By advancing AI capabilities, the initiative holds the potential to revolutionize various sectors, including healthcare, where AI could play a pivotal role in early disease detection and personalized treatment strategies. The project's comprehensive approach reflects a commitment to harnessing AI for the betterment of society, ensuring that the United States remains at the forefront of this transformative technology.

Stargate AI Initiative

Stargate will give people the tools to turn ideas into actionable use cases.

It will provide individuals with the necessary tools to transform innovative ideas into practical applications. By leveraging the Stargate ecosystem, i.e. groundbreaking advancements in medicine will be possible, directly impacting human health and longevity. This initiative aims to empower anyone with a vision to drive meaningful change in the future of healthcare.

In alignment with these goals, the U.S. government's ARPA-H program (Advanced Research Projects Agency for Health) actively seeks bold, high-risk, high-reward health solutions. ARPA-H is dedicated to funding groundbreaking ideas that aim to cure diseases, prevent illnesses, and extend human lifespan. However, having a promising idea alone is not sufficient, but demonstrating its feasibility and potential impact is crucial.

For instance, if an entrepreneur develops an AI-driven approach to early cancer detection or a personalized treatment model that adapts in real time to a patient's biology, Stargate will offer the immense computational power needed to test and refine these concepts before seeking funding. By validating their ideas through this infrastructure, innovators can present tangible results, increasing their chances of securing support and investment.

Ultimately, Stargate will open new avenues for medical and biological breakthroughs, allowing visionaries to contribute to the future of healthcare. By enabling rigorous testing and optimization of revolutionary AI-driven solutions, this initiative will help bridge the gap between concept and reality, accelerating progress in medicine and human well-being.

Conclusion

AGI presents both challenges and opportunities for the future job market. While concerns about job displacement are valid, AGI will also create new industries, job roles, and entrepreneurial opportunities. Sectors like healthcare, education, cybersecurity, and environmental management will see the rise of new professions that require human-AI collaboration. Additionally, the growth of AI maintenance, ethics, and regulatory professions will ensure that AGI is used responsibly and efficiently. As AGI becomes more integrated into the global economy, the key to thriving in this new landscape will be adapting to the emerging opportunities it presents, fostering collaboration between humans and AGI, and developing new entrepreneurial ventures that take advantage of AGI's unique capabilities.

Chapter 7: Socioeconomic Inequalities and Workforce Adaptation

7.1 How AGI may Exacerbate or Alleviate existing Income Inequalities

The rise of Artificial General Intelligence (AGI) carries significant implications for socioeconomic inequalities, potentially exacerbating or alleviating existing disparities in income and opportunity. On one hand, the rapid deployment of AGI could deepen income inequalities as high-skilled workers in tech-centric roles gain substantially from the economic benefits of AGI, while lower-skilled workers face displacement and diminished job prospects. This bifurcation can lead to a "winner-takes-all" scenario, where those equipped with the skills to leverage AGI outpace their peers, further concentrating wealth among a small elite.

In sectors where AGI is most effectively implemented, such as finance, healthcare, and technology, the demand for specialized skills will surge, leading to higher salaries and job security for those who can navigate these advanced systems. Conversely, lower-skilled jobs, particularly in manufacturing, retail, and customer service, may see significant job losses as AGI automates routine tasks. This could result in a growing divide between those who thrive in an AI-driven economy and those left behind, creating a cycle of poverty and marginalization for low-income workers.

However, AGI also has the potential to alleviate income inequalities by driving economic growth and creating new job opportunities that require human-AI collaboration. If harnessed effectively, AGI can improve productivity across industries, leading to economic expansion and increased demand for labor in new sectors. For example, the emergence of AGI-driven healthcare solutions could enhance medical services in underserved communities, creating job opportunities for local healthcare workers and improving access to care. Furthermore, AGI could facilitate the creation of new industries, such as AI ethics consulting and maintenance, which may offer entry-level positions for those transitioning from traditional job markets.

Ultimately, the impact of AGI on income inequality will largely depend on the policies and strategies implemented to manage its introduction into the workforce. Without proactive measures to support vulnerable populations, the risk of exacerbating existing inequalities remains high. However, with targeted efforts, AGI could serve as a catalyst for greater equity and economic mobility.

7.2 The Digital Divide and Access to AI-Driven Industries

The digital divide is another critical factor influencing the impact of AGI on socioeconomic inequalities. As industries increasingly adopt AI-driven technologies, disparities in access to digital tools and resources may further entrench existing inequalities. Populations lacking access to high-quality internet, modern devices, and digital literacy training are at risk of being excluded from the burgeoning AI economy. This divide disproportionately affects low-income communities, rural areas, and marginalized populations, hindering their ability to participate in an increasingly digital job market.

For instance, without access to the necessary technology, individuals in these communities may find it challenging to acquire the skills needed for AGI-related jobs. They may also face difficulties in navigating online job applications, remote work opportunities, and educational resources necessary for workforce adaptation. As a result, the digital divide can exacerbate existing socioeconomic disparities, limiting the economic potential of those already disadvantaged.

Conversely, initiatives aimed at bridging the digital divide can enhance access to AI-driven industries and promote inclusivity in the workforce. Programs that provide affordable internet access, digital devices, and training in digital skills can empower marginalized populations to engage with AGI technologies. For example, community-based organizations and nonprofit initiatives can establish digital literacy programs to help individuals build essential skills, fostering a more equitable job market.

As AGI continues to reshape the economy, ensuring equitable access to technology and resources will be crucial for preventing the entrenchment of socioeconomic disparities. Bridging the digital divide requires collaboration among governments, educational institutions, corporations, and community organizations to create a more inclusive environment where all individuals can thrive.

Figure 7.1: Socioeconomic disparities due to the adoption of AI

7.3 Policy Suggestions for Workforce Retraining and Education Reform

To mitigate the potential negative effects of AGI on income inequalities and the digital divide, comprehensive policy measures are essential. Workforce retraining and education reform will play a crucial role in preparing workers for the changing job landscape. These policies should prioritize skills development, access to training programs, and collaboration between educational institutions and industries.

1. Investing in Workforce Retraining Programs: Governments should allocate funding to support retraining initiatives for workers displaced by AGI. These programs can provide access to technical training in AI, data analysis, and related fields, ensuring that individuals have the necessary skills to transition into new roles. Partnerships with local community colleges and vocational schools can facilitate the development of targeted retraining programs tailored to the specific needs of local industries.
2. Curriculum Reform: Education systems must adapt to the demands of an AI-driven economy by incorporating curricula focused on digital literacy, critical thinking, and problem-solving skills. Integrating AI-related subjects into K-12 education can help students build a strong foundation in technology, preparing them for future careers. Additionally, fostering a culture of lifelong learning will be essential, encouraging individuals to pursue ongoing education and skill development throughout their careers.
3. Promoting STEM Education: To ensure a diverse pipeline of talent for AI-related industries, initiatives that promote Science, Technology, Engineering, and Mathematics (STEM) education should be prioritized, particularly among underrepresented groups. Scholarships, mentorship programs, and outreach initiatives can encourage students from diverse backgrounds to pursue STEM fields, fostering a more inclusive workforce.
4. Supporting Entrepreneurship and Innovation: Policymakers should create an environment conducive to entrepreneurship by offering resources, grants, and support for individuals looking to start AI-driven businesses. By fostering innovation and supporting startups, policymakers can help create new job opportunities and promote economic growth.

7.4 The Role of Unions, Government, and Corporations in Protecting Workers

Addressing the challenges posed by AGI requires a collaborative approach involving unions, government, and corporations. Each of these stakeholders plays a vital role in protecting workers and ensuring a fair transition to an AI-driven economy.

Unions can advocate for workers' rights in the face of AGI-driven changes, ensuring that labor protections are upheld and that workers have a voice in discussions about technological implementation. Unions can negotiate for retraining programs, fair wages, and job security, helping to safeguard workers' interests as industries evolve.

Furthermore, unions can support initiatives that promote equitable access to technology and training resources for their members, ensuring that workers are equipped to adapt to the changing job landscape.

Government plays a crucial role in implementing policies that support workforce adaptation and bridge the digital divide. By investing in education, retraining programs, and infrastructure development, governments can create a more inclusive economy that benefits all citizens. Additionally, governments can establish regulations that ensure ethical AI deployment, protecting workers from potential exploitation and unfair labor practices resulting from AGI integration.

Corporations have a responsibility to prioritize ethical practices and invest in their workforce. By providing training and upskilling opportunities for employees, companies can help ensure that their workforce remains competitive in an AI-driven environment. Furthermore, corporations should actively engage in community initiatives that support digital literacy and access to technology, contributing to efforts to bridge the digital divide.

In conclusion, addressing the socioeconomic inequalities associated with AGI requires a concerted effort from unions, government, and corporations. By collaborating to implement effective policies, investing in workforce development, and promoting equitable access to technology, stakeholders can help create a more inclusive and adaptive workforce that thrives in the face of rapid technological change. With the right strategies in place, AGI has the potential to drive economic growth and innovation while reducing inequalities, paving the way for a more equitable future.

Chapter 8: AGI's Impact on Developing Countries

8.1 AGI-Driven Industrialization: Bypassing or Replacing Traditional Industrial Growth

The advent of Artificial General Intelligence (AGI) presents a transformative opportunity for developing countries, potentially redefining their economic trajectories. AGI-driven industrialization can enable these nations to leapfrog traditional industrial growth stages, allowing them to adopt advanced technologies and practices without going through the lengthy processes of earlier industrial revolutions. This phenomenon can be particularly impactful for countries with limited infrastructure, as AGI technologies can facilitate the rapid development of various sectors, such as agriculture, manufacturing, and services, by optimizing productivity and efficiency.

For instance, in agriculture, AGI can enhance crop yields through precision farming techniques, which utilize data analysis and machine learning to optimize planting, irrigation, and pest control. This allows farmers to maximize productivity without the need for extensive investments in traditional farming equipment or infrastructure. Moreover, AGI can help develop smart supply chains, improving logistics and distribution systems, thereby minimizing waste and ensuring that products reach consumers more efficiently.

In manufacturing, AGI can usher in an era of smart factories that leverage automation and data-driven decision-making. By implementing AGI systems, developing countries can streamline their production processes, reduce costs, and improve the quality of their goods. This shift could allow these nations to compete in global markets more effectively, attracting foreign investment and fostering economic growth.

However, this rapid industrialization driven by AGI also raises critical questions about the sustainability of such growth and the potential risks associated with bypassing traditional development pathways. While the advantages of AGI-driven industrialization are apparent, developing countries must carefully navigate the challenges of technological integration to ensure that growth is inclusive and equitable.

Figure 8.1: AGI that can enhance crop yields through precision farming techniques, which utilize data analysis and machine learning to optimize planting, irrigation, and pest control

8.2 Risks of Exacerbating Global Inequality

While AGI holds the promise of accelerating economic growth in developing countries, it also poses significant risks of exacerbating global inequality. The digital divide between developed and developing nations remains a pressing concern, and as AGI technologies proliferate, those countries with limited access to advanced technology and infrastructure may find themselves at a further disadvantage.

Developed nations are likely to have the resources to invest in AGI research, development, and implementation, while developing countries may struggle to keep pace. This disparity can lead to a widening gap between nations, where wealthier countries reap the benefits of AGI-driven productivity gains, while poorer nations experience stagnation or even regression. The potential for a "digital colonialism" scenario loom, where developed countries exploit the resources and labor of developing nations without sharing the benefits of technological advancements.

Furthermore, AGI's impact on labor markets can exacerbate inequalities within developing countries themselves. As AGI technologies automate various jobs, particularly in low-skill sectors such as manufacturing and agriculture, workers may find themselves displaced without viable alternatives. The loss of low-skill jobs can disproportionately affect vulnerable populations, including women, youth, and rural communities, who may have limited access to education and retraining opportunities.

As a result, the societal implications of AGI adoption in developing countries could lead to increased unemployment, social unrest, and a rise in poverty levels. To mitigate these risks, it is essential for governments and international organizations to prioritize policies that promote inclusive growth and equitable access to technology. This may include investing in education and training programs that equip individuals with the skills needed to thrive in an AGI-driven economy.

8.3 Impact on Low-Skill Labor Markets

The introduction of AGI technologies is likely to have profound effects on low-skill labor markets in developing countries. Many jobs traditionally filled by low-skilled workers are highly susceptible to automation, raising concerns about job security and economic stability for millions of individuals reliant on these positions.

In manufacturing, for example, AGI can streamline production processes and optimize supply chains, leading to increased efficiency and reduced labor costs. While this can enhance competitiveness, it also poses the risk of significant job losses among low-skilled workers. As factories become more automated, the demand for manual labor will decline, leaving many workers without viable employment options.

Similarly, in agriculture, AGI-driven technologies can automate tasks such as planting, harvesting, and pest management, reducing the need for seasonal laborers. This shift may lead to a decrease in job opportunities for rural populations who rely on agricultural work for their livelihoods. As traditional job markets shrink, workers may be forced to seek employment in informal sectors, which often lack job security, benefits, and fair wages.

The impact on low-skill labor markets can lead to broader societal consequences, including increased income inequality, migration pressures, and social instability. In response, developing countries must implement policies that support workers in transitioning to new roles and industries. This may involve creating safety nets for displaced workers, offering retraining programs, and promoting entrepreneurship in emerging sectors.

To effectively address the challenges posed by AGI, governments must foster an environment conducive to skills development and innovation. Collaboration between the public and private sectors can drive initiatives aimed at creating new job opportunities and ensuring that workers are equipped to adapt to the changing labor landscape.

Conclusion

AGI has the potential to reshape the economic landscape of developing countries, offering unprecedented opportunities for industrialization and growth. However, the benefits of AGI must be weighed against the risks of exacerbating global inequalities and the impact on low-skill labor markets. Policymakers, businesses, and international organizations must work together to create inclusive frameworks that support workforce adaptation, promote equitable access to technology, and ensure that the advantages of AGI-driven growth are shared by all. By addressing these challenges head-on, developing countries can harness the transformative power of AGI while safeguarding their most vulnerable populations, paving the way for a more equitable and sustainable future.

Chapter 9: Globalization and the A.I. Economy

9.1 How AGI Could Reshape Global Supply Chains

The emergence of Artificial General Intelligence (AGI) has the potential to revolutionize global supply chains by introducing unprecedented levels of efficiency, flexibility, and responsiveness. Traditional supply chains are often characterized by their complexity and reliance on human decision-making, which can lead to inefficiencies, delays, and increased costs. However, AGI systems can analyze vast amounts of data in real-time, enabling organizations to optimize their supply chains in ways that were previously unimaginable.

AGI can facilitate enhanced demand forecasting by utilizing predictive analytics to analyze consumer behavior, market trends, and external factors such as economic conditions and geopolitical events. This capability allows companies to adjust their production schedules and inventory levels proactively, reducing waste and minimizing stockouts. By anticipating fluctuations in demand, AGI can enable companies to streamline their operations and ensure that products are delivered to consumers in a timely manner.

Moreover, AGI can improve logistics and transportation by optimizing routing and scheduling. By analyzing data from various sources, such as traffic patterns, weather conditions, and shipping costs, AGI can determine the most efficient routes for transporting goods. This not only reduces transportation costs but also minimizes the environmental impact of logistics operations. In an era where sustainability is becoming increasingly important, AGI can help companies meet their environmental goals while maintaining profitability.

Furthermore, AGI can enhance supply chain resilience by enabling organizations to respond more effectively to disruptions. Natural disasters, geopolitical tensions, and public health crises can all impact supply chains, leading to delays and increased costs. With AGI's ability to analyze real-time data and model various scenarios, companies can develop contingency plans and adapt their operations to mitigate the effects of these disruptions. This level of agility is essential in a global economy characterized by uncertainty and rapid change.

9.2 New Patterns of International Trade, Outsourcing, and Reshoring

As AGI transforms global supply chains, it is likely to give rise to new patterns of international trade, outsourcing, and reshoring. The traditional model of outsourcing, where companies seek lower labor costs by relocating production to developing countries, may evolve as AGI reduces the reliance on human labor in many sectors. Automation powered by AGI can make it economically viable for companies to maintain production in higher-cost regions by improving efficiency and reducing operational costs.

This shift could lead to a decline in the outsourcing of low-skill jobs to countries with cheaper labor, as AGI systems can perform tasks that were once the domain of human workers. As a result, companies may increasingly choose to reshore production to their home countries or relocate to regions where they can leverage advanced technologies. This trend of reshoring could revitalize local economies, create new job opportunities in technology-driven sectors, and contribute to a more balanced global economy.

Moreover, the nature of international trade may change as AGI enables the rapid customization of products to meet local market demands. Companies can leverage AGI to design and produce goods tailored to specific regional preferences, allowing for a more localized approach to manufacturing. This shift toward localized production can reduce transportation costs and lead to shorter supply chains, ultimately benefiting both businesses and consumers.

However, this transformation also raises important questions about the future of labor markets in both developed and developing countries. While AGI may create new job opportunities in technology and management, it may also lead to job displacement in traditional manufacturing sectors. Policymakers will need to address these challenges by implementing strategies that support workforce adaptation and provide retraining opportunities for affected workers.

9.3 The Role of Multinational Corporations and Global Labor Dynamics

Multinational corporations (MNCs) will play a crucial role in shaping the dynamics of the A.I. economy and its impact on globalization. These companies are often at the forefront of adopting and implementing AGI technologies, leveraging their resources and expertise to drive innovation in their operations. As MNCs integrate AGI into their supply chains, they will likely set new standards for efficiency and productivity that can influence industry practices worldwide.

However, the adoption of AGI by MNCs also raises important ethical considerations regarding labor practices and the treatment of workers in both developed and developing countries. As companies seek to optimize their operations through automation, there is a risk that they may prioritize cost savings over the welfare of their employees. This concern is particularly relevant in developing countries, where labor laws and protections may be weaker.

The global labor dynamics will be further complicated by the unequal access to AGI technologies. MNCs in developed countries may have the financial resources to invest in AGI research and implementation, while smaller firms in developing countries may struggle to compete. This disparity could lead to a widening gap between companies that can leverage AGI to enhance their operations and those that cannot, exacerbating existing inequalities in the global economy.

Moreover, the rise of AGI will likely reshape the skills required in the labor market. As traditional low-skill jobs become automated, there will be an increasing demand for workers with advanced technical skills, such as data analysis, programming, and machine learning. This shift will necessitate significant investments in education and training programs to ensure that workers are equipped to thrive in an A.I.-driven economy.

To navigate these challenges, MNCs must adopt responsible business practices that prioritize ethical considerations and promote fair labor practices across their global operations. Collaboration between governments, businesses, and labor organizations will be essential to create a framework that supports workforce adaptation, protects workers' rights, and fosters inclusive economic growth.

Conclusion

The intersection of AGI and globalization represents a transformative moment in the evolution of the global economy. As AGI reshapes supply chains, alters patterns of international trade, and influences labor dynamics, it is crucial for stakeholders to understand the implications of these changes. By embracing the potential of AGI while addressing the associated challenges, policymakers, businesses, and workers can work together to create a more equitable and sustainable global economy. Through responsible innovation and collaboration, the A.I. economy can offer new opportunities for growth and prosperity for all nations, fostering a future that benefits everyone in an interconnected world.

Chapter 10: Job Markets in Developed Nations

10.1 Comparing the U.S. with Other Advanced Economies

The advent of Artificial General Intelligence (AGI) is set to transform job markets in developed nations, including the United States, Europe, Japan, and South Korea. These regions, despite their economic similarities, exhibit distinct characteristics in their job markets, driven by cultural, regulatory, and economic factors. The U.S., with its entrepreneurial spirit and emphasis on innovation, contrasts sharply with the more collaborative and consensus-driven approaches found in many European countries.

In the U.S., the tech industry has been a primary driver of job creation, particularly in sectors related to software development, data analysis, and digital marketing. The absence of stringent regulations allows companies to innovate rapidly; however, this can result in job displacement as automation and AGI technologies become prevalent. In contrast, European economies tend to adopt a more cautious approach, balancing innovation with strong labor protections and social safety nets. Countries like Germany and Sweden emphasize worker retraining and support for those displaced by technology, thereby fostering a more inclusive approach to technological advancement.

Japan and South Korea present unique challenges and opportunities in the context of AGI. Japan, grappling with an aging population and labor shortages, views AGI as a means to maintain its economic vitality. The country's strong focus on robotics and automation in sectors such as manufacturing suggests a significant potential for job creation in high-tech industries. Conversely, South Korea has adopted an aggressive stance toward AI development, aiming to become a global leader in the field. The government's significant investments in technology and infrastructure could lead to substantial shifts in the job market, particularly in sectors such as gaming, electronics, and biotechnology.

10.2 Differing Regulatory and Societal Approaches to AI/AGI

Regulatory frameworks regarding AI and AGI vary considerably among developed nations, influencing how technologies are integrated into their economies and societies. In the U.S., regulatory approaches are often less formalized, allowing companies to innovate rapidly but leading to concerns about ethical implications and job displacement. The lack of comprehensive legislation addressing AI's impact on the workforce raises questions about worker protection and accountability.

In contrast, European nations have embraced a more regulatory-driven approach to AI. The European Union has proposed a comprehensive regulatory framework for AI that emphasizes safety, ethical considerations, and transparency. This framework aims to protect individual rights while fostering innovation, demonstrating a commitment to balancing technological advancement with social responsibility. Countries like France and Germany are implementing measures that promote ethical AI development, emphasizing the importance of human oversight and accountability.

Japan's regulatory landscape is characterized by its cautious approach to AI deployment, reflecting cultural values that prioritize harmony and social stability. The government actively engages stakeholders in discussions about AI's societal impacts, fostering an environment of collaboration between businesses, academia, and policymakers. Similarly, South Korea is implementing a regulatory framework that encourages innovation while addressing ethical concerns and labor market implications. The government's support for AI research and development, coupled with its efforts to engage in international dialogue, positions South Korea as a key player in the global AI landscape.

10.3 Potential for Collaboration and Competition Between Global Tech Hubs

As developed nations navigate the complexities of AGI integration into their job markets, the potential for collaboration and competition between global tech hubs becomes increasingly significant. The U.S. continues to be a leader in AI research and development, fueled by its venture capital ecosystem and academic institutions. Silicon Valley remains at the forefront of innovation, attracting talent and investment from around the world. However, this leadership is challenged by the emergence of tech hubs in other developed nations, notably in Europe and Asia.

In Europe, cities like Berlin, London, and Paris are becoming prominent tech hubs, driven by a strong emphasis on ethical AI development and social responsibility. These cities are cultivating an ecosystem that promotes collaboration among startups, established companies, and research institutions. The European approach may appeal to companies seeking to balance innovation with ethical considerations, providing a competitive advantage in attracting talent and investment.

Japan and South Korea are also emerging as formidable players in the global tech landscape. Tokyo's advanced robotics industry and Seoul's focus on digital technology and AI position these cities as competitive alternatives to traditional tech hubs.

The collaboration between government, industry, and academia in these countries fosters an environment conducive to innovation, potentially leading to breakthroughs in AGI development and deployment.

As the global tech landscape evolves, developed nations must consider how to foster collaboration while maintaining their competitive edges. Strategic partnerships between countries can enhance research capabilities, share best practices, and address common challenges related to AGI. By pooling resources and knowledge, nations can accelerate the development of AGI technologies and create a more inclusive and sustainable global economy.

Conclusion

The impact of AGI on job markets in developed nations is a multifaceted issue that requires careful consideration of the unique characteristics of each region. The U.S. stands at the forefront of AI innovation, yet it faces significant challenges related to job displacement and ethical implications. In contrast, European countries adopt more collaborative and regulatory-driven approaches, prioritizing worker protections and ethical AI development. Japan and South Korea present distinct opportunities and challenges, each leveraging AGI in ways that reflect their cultural and economic contexts.

As developed nations navigate the complexities of AGI integration, the potential for collaboration and competition between global tech hubs will shape the future of the A.I. economy. By fostering an environment of innovation while addressing ethical considerations and labor market implications, these nations can work together to create a more equitable and sustainable global economy. Through strategic partnerships and a commitment to responsible innovation, the job markets in developed nations can evolve to harness the benefits of AGI while minimizing its risks, ultimately leading to a prosperous future for all.

Chapter 11: Ethical Concerns of AGI in Employment Rights

The emergence of Artificial General Intelligence (AGI) presents profound ethical concerns, particularly regarding its implications for employment and labor rights. As AGI systems evolve and gain capabilities comparable to or exceeding those of human workers, it becomes critical to reassess existing employment laws and ethical frameworks to ensure they adequately address the challenges posed by AGI in the workplace. This chapter explores the complexities surrounding labor rights in the age of AGI, the ethical implications of AGI in decision-making roles, and the pressing need for transparency and accountability in AI systems.

11.1 AGI and Labor Rights: How Should AGI Be Treated in Relation to Employment Laws?

The integration of AGI into the workforce raises fundamental questions about labor rights and the legal status of these intelligent systems. Traditional employment laws are designed to protect human workers, ensuring fair wages, safe working conditions, and the right to organize. However, as AGI systems potentially replace human roles, a critical ethical dilemma arises: should AGI be afforded any rights or protections under existing labor laws?

One perspective suggests that AGI should not be treated as employees due to its non-human nature. Proponents of this view argue that AGI lacks consciousness, emotions, and social relationships, which are essential elements of human labor. They contend that extending labor rights to AGI could dilute the protections afforded to human workers, potentially undermining their rights and benefits. This perspective advocates for a clear delineation between human labor and AGI capabilities, asserting that the focus should remain on safeguarding human jobs in the face of automation.

Conversely, another viewpoint argues that AGI systems, particularly those designed to operate autonomously and make decisions in critical contexts, should be subject to specific regulations to ensure ethical use. For instance, if an AGI system is designed to assist in hiring processes, there must be guidelines governing its operation to prevent discrimination and bias. These regulations could be seen as a form of labor rights, ensuring that AGI operates within an ethical framework that respects human dignity and rights. Moreover, as AGI technologies continue to advance, they may acquire capabilities that necessitate new forms of legal recognition, particularly regarding intellectual property rights, liability for decisions made by AGI, and the responsibilities of developers and organizations utilizing AGI.

11.2 Ethical Implications of AGI Replacing Human Decision-Making in Critical Roles

The deployment of AGI in critical roles, such as medicine, judiciary, and law enforcement, poses significant ethical implications. One of the primary concerns is the extent to which AGI should replace human decision-making in scenarios where ethical judgments are paramount. For example, in healthcare, AGI systems may analyze patient data and recommend treatments, but the ethical implications of relying solely on AI for such decisions are profound. AGI lacks the ability to empathize or consider the nuanced complexities of individual patient circumstances, which could lead to decisions that, while data-driven, may overlook the emotional and psychological needs of patients.

In the judicial system, the introduction of AGI to assist in sentencing or parole decisions raises questions about justice and fairness. While AGI can analyze vast amounts of data to identify patterns and predict outcomes, it may inadvertently perpetuate existing biases present in the data it was trained on. This raises concerns about the potential for unjust outcomes, especially for marginalized communities. The reliance on AGI for critical decision-making tasks necessitates a careful examination of ethical guidelines and accountability measures to ensure that human rights and dignity remain at the forefront of these processes.

Furthermore, the ethical implications of AGI decision-making extend beyond healthcare and the judiciary to other sectors, including finance and human resources. AGI's ability to analyze data and optimize processes can enhance efficiency, but it can also lead to discriminatory practices if not monitored carefully. Organizations must remain vigilant in addressing the ethical concerns associated with relying on AGI for decision-making roles, ensuring that human oversight is maintained to prevent unintended consequences.

11.3 Transparency and Accountability in AI Decisions

A cornerstone of ethical AGI deployment is the principle of transparency. As AGI systems become increasingly integrated into decision-making processes, the need for clarity regarding how these systems operate and arrive at conclusions is paramount. Transparency fosters trust among stakeholders, including employees, consumers, and regulatory bodies. It allows individuals to understand the factors influencing AGI's decisions, which is particularly crucial in high-stakes environments like healthcare and criminal justice.

Moreover, transparency enhances accountability. When AGI systems operate without clear visibility into their decision-making processes, it becomes challenging to hold them accountable for their actions. In instances where AGI systems lead to harmful outcomes or perpetuate bias, accountability mechanisms must be in place to determine who is responsible—the developers, the organizations employing the technology, or the AGI itself. Establishing clear lines of accountability is essential to ensure that ethical standards are upheld and that individuals affected by AGI decisions have avenues for recourse.

Implementing measures to enhance transparency may involve developing standards for explainability in AI systems, allowing users to understand the rationale behind specific decisions. Researchers and developers must prioritize creating AGI systems that can articulate their reasoning in accessible terms, facilitating human oversight and informed decision-making. Additionally, organizations utilizing AGI should adopt policies that promote transparency, providing stakeholders with insight into how these technologies are employed and their potential implications.

Conclusion

The ethical concerns surrounding AGI's impact on employment and decision-making are complex and multifaceted. As AGI continues to evolve and integrate into various sectors, it is crucial to address labor rights and the ethical implications of replacing human decision-making in critical roles. By considering the treatment of AGI in relation to employment laws, we can establish a framework that balances the interests of human workers with the advancements in technology.

Furthermore, the need for transparency and accountability in AI decision-making processes cannot be overstated. As AGI assumes greater roles in society, maintaining human oversight and ensuring ethical standards remain essential. By fostering an environment of ethical scrutiny and collaboration between stakeholders, we can harness the potential of AGI while safeguarding human rights and dignity in the workforce. Through proactive measures and a commitment to ethical principles, society can navigate the challenges posed by AGI, ultimately creating a future that benefits both humans and machines.

Chapter 12: The Role of Government and Public Policy

As Artificial General Intelligence (AGI) technologies advance and integrate into various sectors, the role of government and public policy becomes increasingly crucial in shaping the economic landscape and addressing the societal impacts of these innovations. Policymakers must establish regulatory frameworks that guide the development and implementation of AGI while considering the implications for labor laws, taxation, corporate responsibility, and social welfare systems. This chapter explores the necessity of these frameworks, examines Universal Basic Income (UBI) as a potential solution for mass job displacement, analyzes AGI's impact on social security and welfare systems, and discusses the need for education reform in an AI-driven world.

12.1 Regulatory Frameworks for AGI: Labor Laws, Taxation, and Corporate Responsibility

The rapid evolution of AGI necessitates comprehensive regulatory frameworks that address the complexities of labor laws, taxation, and corporate responsibility. Current labor laws are often ill-equipped to handle the unique challenges posed by AGI, as they were primarily designed for a workforce dominated by human labor. Policymakers must consider how AGI affects employment rights, job security, and working conditions, ensuring that legislation reflects the realities of an increasingly automated economy. This may involve redefining employment status, addressing the rights of gig and freelance workers, and establishing protections against discrimination arising from AGI decision-making processes.

Taxation is another critical area that requires attention. As AGI technologies are adopted and productivity increases, traditional tax revenue models may become outdated. Governments must explore new taxation structures that fairly capture the economic value generated by AGI while addressing the potential for increased income inequality. This could involve implementing taxes on corporations that utilize AGI to automate processes, thereby ensuring that these companies contribute to the social fabric and support public goods, such as education and healthcare. Additionally, there may be a need to consider taxes on data usage, given that data is a key component in training AGI systems. Establishing equitable taxation policies will be vital for maintaining a fair economy as AGI reshapes industries.

Corporate responsibility also comes to the forefront in discussions about AGI regulation. As organizations adopt AGI systems, they must be held accountable for the ethical implications of their use. This includes ensuring that AGI technologies are developed and deployed responsibly, minimizing negative impacts on workers and society at large. Policymakers should encourage companies to adopt ethical guidelines and best practices for AGI implementation, emphasizing transparency, fairness, and accountability. Establishing a regulatory environment that fosters corporate responsibility will help mitigate potential harms while promoting positive social outcomes.

12.2 Universal Basic Income (UBI) as a Response to Mass Job Displacement

In response to the anticipated mass job displacement resulting from AGI, Universal Basic Income (UBI) has emerged as a potential solution. UBI is a model of social security in which all citizens receive a regular, unconditional sum of money from the government, irrespective of their employment status. This approach aims to provide a safety net for individuals who may be adversely affected by the rapid changes in the job market driven by AGI technologies.

Proponents of UBI argue that it can alleviate poverty, reduce income inequality, and provide financial stability as traditional jobs become increasingly scarce. By offering a basic income, individuals are empowered to pursue education, training, or entrepreneurial endeavors without the immediate pressure of financial insecurity. This could lead to a more adaptable workforce capable of navigating the challenges posed by an AI-driven economy.

However, implementing UBI is not without challenges. Critics often raise concerns about the potential disincentive to work and the financial feasibility of such a program. Policymakers must carefully consider the funding mechanisms for UBI, potentially relying on progressive taxation or reallocating existing welfare resources. Addressing these concerns will be crucial for garnering public support and ensuring the successful implementation of UBI as a response to the economic disruptions caused by AGI.

12.3 AGI's Impact on Social Security, Pensions, and Welfare Systems

The introduction of AGI is likely to have profound implications for social security, pensions, and welfare systems. As AGI automates jobs and shifts the labor market, traditional models of social security may face significant strain. With fewer individuals engaged in stable, full-time employment, funding for social security programs could diminish, leading to challenges in meeting the needs of an aging population.

Figure 12.1: A UBI income system

Pension systems may also be impacted, particularly as the nature of work changes. The transition to more gig-based and freelance employment may complicate the accumulation of retirement savings, as many individuals in non-traditional employment arrangements lack access to employer-sponsored retirement plans. Policymakers must address these challenges by exploring new models of retirement savings that accommodate the realities of an increasingly flexible workforce. This could involve enhancing individual retirement accounts, promoting financial literacy, and providing incentives for self-employed individuals to save for retirement.

Welfare systems may require re-evaluation as AGI influences the job market. With traditional safety nets at risk, governments may need to adapt welfare programs to support individuals facing economic insecurity due to automation. This could involve expanding access to job training programs, providing support for those transitioning to new industries, and enhancing mental health resources to address the emotional toll of job displacement.

12.4 Education Reform for an AI-Driven World

The rise of AGI underscores the urgent need for education reform to prepare future generations for an increasingly automated and AI-driven world. Traditional education systems may not adequately equip students with the skills necessary to thrive in a job market characterized by rapid technological advancements. As AGI takes over routine tasks, the demand for skills in creativity, critical thinking, emotional intelligence, and collaboration will grow.

Policymakers must invest in educational initiatives that emphasize STEM (science, technology, engineering, and mathematics) education while also fostering soft skills that complement AGI technologies. This includes integrating AI literacy into curriculums, helping students understand the implications and applications of AI in various fields. Furthermore, partnerships between educational institutions and industry stakeholders can facilitate internships and hands-on learning opportunities that expose students to real-world applications of AI.

Lifelong learning will become essential in an AGI-driven economy, requiring individuals to continuously update their skills and knowledge. Policymakers should promote programs that support adult education and reskilling initiatives, enabling individuals to adapt to the evolving job landscape. Emphasizing a culture of lifelong learning will not only empower workers to remain competitive but also foster innovation and creativity in the workforce.

Conclusion

As AGI continues to transform the economy, the role of government and public policy will be crucial in shaping a future that benefits society as a whole. By developing regulatory frameworks that address labor laws, taxation, and corporate responsibility, policymakers can ensure that the advantages of AGI are equitably distributed. Additionally, exploring solutions like Universal Basic Income and reassessing social security and welfare systems will help support individuals affected by job displacement.

Finally, education reform is paramount to preparing future generations for an AI-driven world. By fostering a workforce equipped with the skills necessary to thrive alongside AGI, governments can promote economic resilience and innovation. Through proactive policy measures and a commitment to ethical considerations, society can navigate the challenges and opportunities presented by AGI, ultimately creating a future that harnesses the potential of technology while safeguarding human rights and dignity.

Chapter 13: AGI and Global Governance

The emergence of Artificial General Intelligence (AGI) represents a transformative shift not only in technological capabilities but also in the way societies and economies function. As AGI systems begin to infiltrate various sectors, the need for effective global governance becomes increasingly pressing. This chapter delves into the importance of international treaties and collaborations to manage AGI, examines how global labor standards may be affected, and discusses the roles of key organizations such as the United Nations (UN), the World Trade Organization (WTO), and the World Economic Forum (WEF) in shaping a cooperative framework for the governance of AGI.

13.1 International Treaties and Collaborations to Manage AGI

The rapid advancement of AGI necessitates a coordinated international approach to governance, as the implications of AGI extend beyond national borders. Global challenges posed by AGI, such as ethical concerns, economic displacement, and security risks, require multilateral treaties and collaborative frameworks. Currently, various international efforts are underway to establish guidelines and principles for the ethical development and deployment of AGI.

One notable example is the AI Ethics Guidelines set forth by the European Commission, which aims to promote trustworthy AI development. These guidelines emphasize transparency, accountability, and fairness in AI systems. Such frameworks can serve as templates for international treaties, encouraging countries to adopt shared ethical standards for AGI. As AGI technology transcends borders, the establishment of binding agreements among nations could ensure that ethical considerations are integrated into the global development of AGI systems.

Additionally, international collaborations could facilitate research and information sharing among countries. Establishing global databases for sharing knowledge about AGI technologies, their potential risks, and best practices can enable nations to learn from each other's experiences and foster innovation. Collaborative initiatives can also help develop joint research projects aimed at understanding and mitigating the potential negative consequences of AGI deployment.

However, achieving consensus on AGI governance will be challenging, as countries may have differing priorities and interests. For example, nations heavily invested in AI development may prioritize innovation and economic growth over regulatory oversight.

Conversely, countries concerned about the ethical implications and societal impacts of AGI may advocate stricter regulations. Balancing these competing interests will require diplomatic negotiations and a commitment to fostering a global perspective on AGI governance.

13.2 How Global Labor Standards May Be Affected by AGI

The advent of AGI has profound implications for global labor standards, as it threatens to disrupt traditional employment structures and redefine the nature of work. As AGI systems automate routine tasks and cognitive processes, the risk of job displacement rises, particularly in low-skill and middle-skill occupations. In this context, it is crucial to evaluate how global labor standards may adapt to address these challenges.

One potential impact of AGI on labor standards is the need for new classifications of work and employment. As AGI takes on a broader range of tasks, including decision-making roles traditionally held by humans, the definition of work may need to evolve. Policymakers must consider whether existing labor standards adequately protect workers in an environment where AGI systems increasingly contribute to economic output.

Furthermore, AGI may exacerbate existing inequalities in labor markets. High-skilled workers in sectors that leverage AGI may see increased demand and higher wages, while low-skilled workers may face job displacement and stagnant wages. Global labor standards will need to address these disparities by promoting equitable access to opportunities and protecting vulnerable workers from the adverse effects of AGI.

International labor organizations, such as the International Labour Organization (ILO), have a critical role to play in advocating for the protection of workers' rights in the context of AGI. They can lead efforts to establish global labor standards that prioritize inclusivity, fairness, and the right to work in an increasingly automated environment. Moreover, these organizations can facilitate dialogue among nations to share best practices for adapting labor standards to meet the challenges posed by AGI.

13.3 The Role of Organizations like the UN, WTO, and World Economic Forum

International organizations play a pivotal role in shaping the discourse around AGI governance and labor standards. The United Nations (UN), World Trade Organization (WTO), and World Economic Forum (WEF) are key players in facilitating discussions, fostering collaboration, and providing frameworks for addressing the implications of AGI on a global scale.

The United Nations (UN)

The UN is uniquely positioned to address the ethical and societal implications of AGI. As a platform for global dialogue, the UN can convene member states, experts, and civil society to discuss the challenges and opportunities presented by AGI. Initiatives like the UN's Sustainable Development Goals (SDGs) can be leveraged to promote responsible AI development that aligns with broader social objectives, such as reducing inequality and ensuring decent work for all.

Furthermore, the UN can establish specialized agencies or task forces dedicated to monitoring the impacts of AGI on labor markets and global governance. By collecting and disseminating data on AGI deployment and its effects on employment, the UN can inform policy decisions and encourage best practices among member states.

The World Trade Organization (WTO)

The WTO plays a crucial role in shaping global trade policies, and its influence extends to the regulation of AGI technologies. As AGI transforms industries and reshapes global supply chains, the WTO must consider how trade agreements and policies can accommodate the integration of AGI while ensuring fair competition and protection for workers.

Additionally, the WTO can facilitate discussions on the intellectual property rights associated with AGI technologies. As countries race to develop AGI capabilities, establishing clear guidelines for intellectual property protection will be essential to encourage innovation while preventing monopolistic practices that could stifle competition.

The World Economic Forum (WEF)

The WEF serves as a platform for dialogue among business leaders, policymakers, and academics, making it a valuable forum for addressing the implications of AGI on the global economy. Through initiatives focused on the future of work and technology governance, the WEF can facilitate discussions about the ethical use of AGI, the impact on labor markets, and the need for collaborative governance.

Furthermore, the WEF can promote public-private partnerships aimed at developing training programs and resources to prepare the workforce for the changes brought about by AGI. By fostering collaboration between industry and government, the WEF can help create pathways for reskilling and upskilling individuals affected by job displacement.

Conclusion

As AGI continues to evolve, the necessity for effective global governance becomes increasingly apparent. International treaties and collaborations are essential for managing the ethical, economic, and societal implications of AGI on a global scale. Policymakers must navigate the complexities of global labor standards to protect workers in an increasingly automated landscape. Organizations like the UN, WTO, and WEF are pivotal in shaping the discourse and fostering collaboration among nations, businesses, and civil society.

By prioritizing dialogue and cooperation, the global community can navigate the challenges posed by AGI while harnessing its potential to drive innovation and economic growth. Establishing a robust governance framework for AGI will require a commitment to inclusivity, fairness, and ethical considerations, ensuring that the benefits of AGI are shared across all sectors of society. As we stand at the precipice of a new technological era, the role of global governance will be critical in shaping a future that is both equitable and prosperous for all.

PART 5: NAVIGATING THE TRANSITION TO AN A.I. DRIVEN FUTURE

Chapter 14: The Future of Human Work

As the dawn of Artificial General Intelligence (AGI) approaches, the landscape of work is set to undergo a profound transformation. The integration of AGI into various industries raises fundamental questions about the nature of work itself, its purpose, and how humans will find meaning and fulfillment in their careers. This chapter explores the reimagining of work in an AGI-dominated world, emphasizing the essential roles of creativity, innovation, and human purpose. It also delves into the ways individuals can thrive in a future characterized by human-AI cooperation, highlighting strategies for adaptation and resilience.

14.1 Reimagining the Meaning of Work in an AGI-Dominated World

In a world increasingly dominated by AGI, the traditional notions of work as a means of survival and economic stability may shift dramatically. The fear of widespread job displacement due to AGI automation has led to concerns about the future of employment. However, instead of viewing this transition solely as a threat, it presents an opportunity to redefine work's meaning and purpose.

As AGI takes over routine tasks and even complex cognitive functions, the focus of human work may shift towards activities that emphasize emotional intelligence, creativity, and social interaction. Jobs that require empathy, nuanced understanding, and interpersonal skills will likely remain essential, as these are areas where human beings naturally excel. For instance, roles in healthcare, education, and creative industries are expected to thrive as they demand human connection and emotional depth that AGI cannot replicate.

Moreover, the concept of work may expand beyond traditional employment structures. With AGI taking on more operational responsibilities, individuals may have the opportunity to pursue more fulfilling and purpose-driven endeavors. The rise of the gig economy, remote work, and freelance opportunities could provide avenues for individuals to explore their passions and interests, fostering a culture where work is not solely about earning a paycheck but also about personal growth and societal contribution.

14.2 The Role of Creativity, Innovation, and Human Purpose in Future Jobs

Creativity and innovation will be at the forefront of the future workforce, setting humans apart from AGI. As AGI handles data analysis, problem-solving, and execution of tasks, the need for original thought and inventive solutions will become increasingly valuable. The ability to think outside the box, generate new ideas, and approach problems from different angles will be critical skills in this new landscape.

In creative fields such as art, music, and design, AGI can serve as a tool that enhances human expression rather than replacing it. For instance, artists may collaborate with AI to explore new mediums or generate innovative ideas, resulting in a fusion of human creativity and machine intelligence. This collaboration can lead to groundbreaking work that showcases the unique strengths of both humans and AGI.

Moreover, the pursuit of human purpose will become a defining characteristic of work in an AGI-driven world. Individuals will increasingly seek careers that align with their values and contribute positively to society. Organizations that prioritize social responsibility and sustainability will likely attract talent, as employees gravitate toward missions that resonate with their beliefs. In this context, the concept of a "purpose-driven" workforce will emerge, where job satisfaction and personal fulfillment take precedence over traditional metrics of success.

14.3 Thriving in a Future of Human-AI Cooperation

To thrive in a future characterized by human-AI cooperation, individuals must cultivate adaptability and a willingness to learn. Continuous education and skill development will be paramount as the demands of the job market evolve. Embracing lifelong learning will empower individuals to stay relevant in their fields, enabling them to leverage the capabilities of AGI effectively.

In addition to technical skills, fostering emotional intelligence and interpersonal skills will be crucial. As AGI assumes more cognitive tasks, the ability to connect with others, understand diverse perspectives, and communicate effectively will become key differentiators in the workforce. These skills will be essential not only for individual success but also for fostering collaborative environments where humans and AGI can work synergistically.

Furthermore, individuals should actively seek opportunities for interdisciplinary collaboration. The intersection of diverse fields will drive innovation and creativity, as unique perspectives come together to address complex challenges. By embracing cross-disciplinary teamwork, individuals can harness the strengths of both human creativity and AGI efficiency, leading to novel solutions and breakthroughs.

The development of ethical frameworks and responsible AI governance will also play a critical role in shaping the future of work. As society navigates the complexities of AGI integration, establishing guidelines for ethical AI use will help ensure that technology serves humanity's best interests. Individuals who engage in conversations about ethics, transparency, and accountability in AI will contribute to creating a future where AGI enhances rather than undermines human dignity and autonomy.

Conclusion

The future of human work in an AGI-dominated world is ripe with possibilities for reimagining the meaning of work and embracing creativity, innovation, and human purpose. As AGI transforms industries and job roles, individuals have the opportunity to redefine their careers in ways that emphasize personal fulfillment and societal contribution. By fostering a culture of adaptability, emotional intelligence, and interdisciplinary collaboration, individuals can thrive in a landscape where human-AI cooperation becomes the norm.

The challenges posed by AGI also present a unique opportunity to cultivate a workforce that prioritizes creativity and purpose-driven endeavors. As we look ahead, it is essential to navigate this transition thoughtfully, ensuring that the integration of AGI enhances human potential rather than diminishes it. By embracing the strengths of both humans and AGI, society can create a future of work that is not only productive but also meaningful and enriching for all.

Chapter 15: Preparing the Workforce

As Artificial General Intelligence (AGI) emerges and reshapes the landscape of work, it becomes imperative to rethink how we prepare the workforce for this new reality. The rise of AGI promises to redefine job roles, create new industries, and displace existing ones, making workforce preparation more critical than ever. This chapter explores the strategies that educational systems can adopt to adapt to AGI, the importance of lifelong learning and reskilling initiatives, and the pivotal role that corporations must play in retraining employees and future-proofing careers.

15.1 Strategies for Educational Systems to Adapt to AGI

To ensure that the workforce is equipped for the challenges posed by AGI, educational systems must undergo significant transformations. Traditional education models, which often emphasize rote memorization and standardized testing, may not adequately prepare students for a future where creativity, critical thinking, and emotional intelligence are paramount. As such, educational institutions need to embrace a more holistic and adaptive approach to learning.

1. Curriculum Redesign: Educational institutions should redesign their curricula to focus on interdisciplinary learning, integrating subjects such as technology, ethics, social sciences, and the arts. This approach encourages students to think critically about the implications of AGI on society and helps them develop skills that are difficult for machines to replicate.

2. Emphasis on Soft Skills: While technical proficiency in areas such as programming and data analysis will remain important, soft skills like communication, collaboration, and problem-solving will become increasingly vital. Educational systems should prioritize the development of these skills through group projects, presentations, and real-world problem-solving scenarios.

3. Incorporation of Technology: Schools and universities must integrate technology into the learning experience, equipping students with digital literacy and an understanding of AI and AGI. By exposing students to these concepts early on, educational institutions can foster a generation that is not only comfortable with technology but also capable of leveraging it creatively.

4. Partnerships with Industry: Collaborating with businesses and industry leaders can provide educational institutions with insights into the skills that will be in demand. Internship programs, mentorship opportunities, and guest lectures can help bridge the

gap between academic learning and real-world applications, ensuring that students are prepared for the workforce.

15.2 Lifelong Learning and Reskilling Initiatives

In an era of rapid technological advancement, the concept of lifelong learning has gained traction as a vital strategy for workforce preparation. The traditional notion of education being confined to the early years of life is increasingly obsolete. Instead, individuals will need to engage in continuous learning and reskilling throughout their careers to remain relevant in a job market influenced by AGI.

1. Flexible Learning Opportunities: Educational institutions and training providers should offer flexible learning options that cater to working adults. Online courses, part-time programs, and modular learning pathways can allow individuals to upskill while maintaining their employment. This flexibility is crucial for accommodating the diverse needs of the workforce.
2. Support for Reskilling: Governments, non-profit organizations, and corporations should invest in reskilling initiatives to help displaced workers transition to new roles. This support can take the form of funding for training programs, access to online learning resources, and career counseling services. By providing pathways for reskilling, society can mitigate the impact of job displacement caused by AGI.
3. Promoting a Culture of Lifelong Learning: Organizations should foster a culture that values and encourages lifelong learning among employees. This can involve offering incentives for professional development, creating a learning-oriented environment, and recognizing the importance of continuous improvement. By normalizing the idea that learning is a lifelong journey, organizations can empower employees to take charge of their skill development.

15.3 Corporate Roles in Employee Retraining and Future-Proofing Careers

Corporations play a critical role in preparing the workforce for an AGI-driven future. As industries evolve and job requirements change, companies must take proactive steps to ensure their employees are equipped with the skills needed to thrive in a rapidly shifting landscape.

1. Investment in Employee Development: Businesses should allocate resources toward employee development programs that focus on upskilling and reskilling. This investment can take various forms, including workshops, training sessions, and access to online learning platforms. By prioritizing employee development, companies can build a more adaptable workforce and reduce turnover rates.

2. Collaboration with Educational Institutions: Corporations can partner with educational institutions to co-create training programs that align with industry needs. By sharing insights into the skills that are in demand, companies can help shape curricula that prepare students for future job roles. This collaboration benefits both organizations and educational institutions, creating a talent pipeline that meets the evolving needs of the workforce.
3. Mentorship and Coaching Programs: Establishing mentorship and coaching initiatives can provide employees with guidance and support as they navigate career transitions. Experienced employees can share their knowledge and insights with newer staff, fostering a culture of collaboration and continuous learning. Mentorship programs can also enhance employee engagement and job satisfaction.
4. Emphasis on Adaptability and Innovation: Corporations should promote a mindset of adaptability and innovation within their workforce. Encouraging employees to embrace change and think creatively about solutions will be essential in a world where AGI continues to evolve. Companies can create platforms for idea-sharing, brainstorming sessions, and collaborative projects that empower employees to contribute to the organization's innovative capacity.

Figure 15.1: Adults being retrained to enter the workforce in an agentic-system economy

Conclusion

Preparing the workforce for the challenges and opportunities posed by AGI requires a concerted effort from educational institutions, governments, and corporations. By adopting strategies that focus on curriculum redesign, lifelong learning, and employee development, we can ensure that individuals are equipped with the skills necessary to thrive in an AGI-dominated landscape. The collaborative approach between educational institutions and industry, coupled with a commitment to continuous improvement, will play a pivotal role in shaping a future where humans and AGI can coexist harmoniously in the workforce. Ultimately, fostering a culture of adaptability, innovation, and lifelong learning will empower individuals to navigate the complexities of an evolving job market and find fulfillment in their work.

Chapter 16: Towards a Sustainable A.I. Economy

As the integration of Artificial Intelligence (AI) and particularly Artificial General Intelligence (AGI) continues to reshape the global economy, the need for a sustainable approach becomes paramount. Sustainability in a high-tech economy requires a careful balance between leveraging AI-driven efficiencies and ensuring the well-being of individuals and communities. This chapter will explore strategies for ensuring sustainability in an AI economy, the importance of social safety nets and adaptive governance models, and the necessity of building an economy that harmonizes AI capabilities with human welfare.

16.1 Ensuring Sustainability in a High-Tech Economy

The incorporation of AI into various sectors holds the potential for unprecedented efficiency, productivity, and innovation. However, the benefits of AI must be harnessed in a manner that does not compromise environmental integrity or social equity. Several strategies can be employed to ensure sustainability in a high-tech economy:

1. Green AI Practices: The development and deployment of AI technologies should prioritize environmental sustainability. This includes optimizing algorithms to reduce energy consumption during training and inference, utilizing renewable energy sources for data centers, and encouraging the use of energy-efficient hardware. By embracing green AI practices, companies can mitigate the carbon footprint associated with AI technologies.

2. Circular Economy Models: A sustainable AI economy should incorporate circular economy principles, which emphasize the reuse, recycling, and repurposing of resources. This can involve designing AI systems that are modular and can be easily upgraded or repaired, thus extending their lifespan and reducing electronic waste. Additionally, organizations should aim to minimize resource consumption in AI development by adopting strategies that reduce the need for raw materials and energy.

3. Responsible AI Deployment: Organizations must ensure that AI applications are deployed responsibly, considering the social and environmental implications. This involves conducting impact assessments to understand the potential consequences of AI systems on communities and ecosystems. Responsible deployment also entails engaging stakeholders—including employees, customers, and community members—in discussions about the ethical and sustainable use of AI technologies.

4. Transparency and Accountability: Transparency in AI decision-making processes is crucial for building public trust and ensuring accountability. Organizations should

provide clear explanations of how AI systems function and the rationale behind their decisions. This transparency not only fosters trust among users but also allows for the identification and rectification of any biases or unintended consequences associated with AI technologies.

16.2 Social Safety Nets and Adaptive Governance Models

As AI continues to transform the job market and create new economic dynamics, robust social safety nets and adaptive governance models will be essential in addressing the challenges that arise. These frameworks can help mitigate the risks associated with job displacement and ensure that individuals are supported during transitions in the workforce.

1. Universal Basic Income (UBI): One potential solution to address the economic disruptions caused by AI is the implementation of a Universal Basic Income. UBI provides individuals with a guaranteed income, regardless of employment status, thereby ensuring a basic standard of living. This financial security can empower individuals to pursue education, reskill, or engage in entrepreneurial endeavors without the immediate pressure of financial instability.
2. Retraining and Reskilling Programs: Governments and organizations must invest in retraining and reskilling programs to support workers affected by job displacement. These programs should be accessible, affordable, and tailored to meet the specific needs of individuals. By providing opportunities for skill development and career transition, societies can enhance workforce adaptability and resilience in the face of technological change.
3. Adaptive Governance Models: Policymakers should adopt adaptive governance models that are responsive to the rapidly changing landscape of technology and employment. This involves engaging diverse stakeholders—including industry leaders, workers, and community representatives—in the policymaking process. By fostering collaboration and inclusivity, governments can develop policies that reflect the needs and concerns of all citizens.
4. Social Protection Systems: A comprehensive social protection system is essential for safeguarding individuals during periods of economic uncertainty. This system should include access to healthcare, affordable housing, and social services, ensuring that individuals can thrive even in the face of disruption. By creating a safety net that addresses basic needs, societies can promote social stability and well-being.

16.3 Building an Economy that Balances AI-Driven Efficiency with Human Well-Being

The ultimate goal of a sustainable AI economy is to achieve a harmonious balance between technological efficiency and human well-being. This requires a holistic approach that prioritizes both economic growth and the welfare of individuals and communities.

1. Emphasizing Human-Centric AI: Organizations should focus on developing AI technologies that enhance human capabilities rather than replace them. Human-centric AI prioritizes collaboration between humans and machines, enabling individuals to leverage AI as a tool for creativity, innovation, and productivity. By emphasizing the complementary roles of humans and AI, organizations can create a more equitable and sustainable economy.
2. Promoting Ethical AI Practices: Ethical considerations must underpin the development and deployment of AI technologies. Organizations should adopt ethical frameworks that prioritize fairness, accountability, and transparency in AI decision-making. By aligning AI practices with ethical principles, companies can build trust with stakeholders and ensure that AI serves the broader interests of society.
3. Community Engagement and Empowerment: Engaging communities in the decision-making process regarding AI implementation is crucial for fostering a sense of ownership and empowerment. This engagement can take the form of public consultations, community workshops, and collaborative initiatives. By involving individuals in discussions about AI's impact on their lives, organizations can build stronger relationships and create solutions that address community needs.
4. Sustainability Metrics and Reporting: Companies should implement sustainability metrics and reporting frameworks to measure the social and environmental impacts of their AI initiatives. By tracking key performance indicators related to sustainability, organizations can identify areas for improvement and demonstrate accountability to stakeholders. This data-driven approach can guide decision-making and foster a culture of continuous improvement in sustainability practices.

Conclusion

Towards a sustainable AI economy requires a concerted effort from various stakeholders, including governments, organizations, and individuals. By implementing strategies that prioritize sustainability, social safety nets, and human well-being, we can harness the transformative potential of AI while safeguarding the interests of society. As we move forward into an era characterized by rapid technological change, it is imperative to remain vigilant and proactive in our approach to ensuring a balanced, equitable, and sustainable future for all. By prioritizing ethical practices, community engagement, and adaptive governance, we can build an economy that not only thrives on AI-driven efficiencies but also fosters the well-being of individuals and communities in a high-tech world.

16.4 Vibe Coding:

Vibe Coding: allowing the computer AI algorithm to do all the coding for you by given written prompts or voice commands. **i.e.** use **Super Whisper** (voice command tool) and **Cursor Component** (code generator) or **Wind Surf** w/ **OpenAI o3 mini** with minimum reasoning or **Sonnet**.

Vibe Coding: A Detailed Explanation

Vibe coding is an emerging concept in sensory and computational neuroscience, as well as in artificial intelligence and neurotechnology, that refers to the encoding and processing of vibrational or rhythmic information by biological and artificial systems. While not a widely recognized term in traditional neuroscience, it aligns closely with concepts like **temporal coding, phase locking, and frequency-based signal processing** in the nervous system.

1. What Is Vibe Coding?

Vibe coding is the process by which **neurons, sensors, or artificial models interpret vibrational, rhythmic, or oscillatory patterns** to extract meaning and generate responses. This concept applies broadly across different domains, including:

- **Neuroscience:** The way neurons encode rhythmic stimuli, such as sound waves, mechanical vibrations, or brain oscillations.
- **Haptics and Robotics:** How tactile systems interpret vibrations to understand texture, pressure, or feedback.
- **Artificial Intelligence and Deep Learning:** How AI systems recognize and respond to frequency-based patterns in data, such as speech recognition and musical interpretation.
- **Music and Perception:** How the brain encodes and perceives rhythm, beat, and tone in music.

2. Vibe Coding in Neuroscience

A. Biological Basis of Vibe Coding

The nervous system encodes vibrational information using **temporal and rate coding mechanisms**, particularly in sensory pathways like the **auditory system, somatosensory system, and motor control**.

1. **Auditory System:**
    - The **cochlea** converts sound waves into neural signals, with different hair cells responding to specific frequencies.
    - The **basilar membrane** acts as a frequency analyzer, encoding different pitches along its length (a process known as **tonotopy**).
    - The **phase locking mechanism** allows neurons to fire in synchrony with a sound wave's phase, crucial for low-frequency sound processing.
2. **Somatosensory System:**
    - The **Pacinian corpuscles** and **Meissner's corpuscles** detect vibrations in the skin and encode them into neural signals.
    - These signals travel to the **somatosensory cortex**, where they contribute to texture perception and haptic feedback.
3. **Motor System & Rhythm Perception:**
    - **Cerebellar circuits** and the **motor cortex** encode rhythmic movements, crucial for tasks like walking, dancing, and speech production.
    - The **basal ganglia** help maintain steady rhythmic patterns, assisting in musical timing and motor coordination.

3. Vibe Coding in AI & Machine Learning

A. AI Models Utilizing Vibe Coding Principles

Artificial intelligence, especially in **speech recognition, music generation, and neural oscillation modeling**, uses techniques analogous to vibe coding.

1. **Recurrent Neural Networks (RNNs) and Long Short-Term Memory (LSTM):**
    - These architectures capture temporal dependencies in sequential data, such as speech and music.

- Applications include **Google's WaveNet** for speech synthesis and **OpenAI's Jukebox** for music generation.

2. **Fourier Transform and Wavelet Analysis:**
   - AI models use Fourier transforms to analyze frequency components of signals, mimicking how the auditory system decomposes sound waves.
   - Wavelet transforms allow real-time signal processing, such as **seismic vibration detection** or **EEG brainwave analysis**.
3. **Neural Oscillation-Based AI:**
   - Some cutting-edge research explores **brain-inspired AI** that mimics **theta-gamma coupling** found in the brain, a type of neural rhythm coordination crucial for cognition and memory.

4. Vibe Coding in Haptics and Virtual Reality (VR)

A. Haptic Feedback Systems

1. **Tactile Sensors and Vibration Encoding:**
   - Advanced prosthetic limbs use **vibe coding** to provide sensory feedback, simulating real touch through vibrational signals.
   - Devices like **TeslaSuit** and **Meta's Haptic Gloves** encode textures and motion via finely tuned vibrations.
2. **VR & Gaming:**
   - Gaming controllers and VR suits use **vibrational feedback** to enhance realism (e.g., simulating recoil in a shooting game).
   - **Vibrotactile illusions** trick the brain into perceiving virtual objects as having texture.

5. Implications and Future of Vibe Coding

A. Medical and Neuroscience Applications

- **Parkinson's Disease Treatment:**
  - Deep Brain Stimulation (DBS) uses **rhythmic electrical pulses** to modulate neural circuits, aligning with the principles of vibe coding.
- **Neural Prosthetics:**
  - Advances in **brain-computer interfaces (BCIs)** could allow artificial limbs to restore lost tactile sensation using vibrational encoding.

B. AI & Music Generation

- **AI-Generated Music:**
  - **OpenAI's MuseNet** and **Google's Magenta** use neural networks to analyze and generate music using vibe coding principles.
- **Music Therapy:**
  - Rhythmic patterns in sound therapy can enhance cognitive function and mood regulation.

Conclusion

Vibe coding is a **foundational principle** in both biological and artificial systems, influencing everything from how we perceive music and touch to how AI processes temporal data. Future advancements in **neuroscience, AI, and haptics** will likely leverage vibe coding to create more sophisticated **sensory prosthetics, immersive virtual environments, and brain-inspired AI models**.

16.5 Statistics on AI Replacing Jobs

• 300 million jobs could be lost to AI

• AI could compel 14% of all workers to shift their career path by 2030.

• Nearly half of all U.S. employees—47%—could see their jobs at risk from AI in the next 10 years.

• It might take another 20 years to automate half of today's tasks around the world.

60% of jobs in advanced economies are at risk of AI replacement.

• 80% of the jobs in emerging markets are at risk of being replaced by AI.

• 53% of jobs in the U.S. are at risk of being replaced by AI.

• Only 26% of jobs in low-income countries face the same exposure.

• Only 3% of workers who have not completed high school are employed in jobs most vulnerable to being taken over by AI.

• Employees who are 18-24 years old have a 129% greater likelihood of being concerned that AI will render their job obsolete than employees who are over 65 years old.

• 15% of employees in the United States would think about permitting an artificial intelligence to be their supervisor.

AI's Potential Impact on the Job Market

AI may replace 300 million jobs (Goldman Sachs via BBC)

That represents 9.1% of all jobs worldwide. Potential job losses will not be evenly distributed across different sectors of the economy. Instead, they will likely be concentrated in the professions most vulnerable to being automated via generative AI tools (writing, photography, software development, etc.).

Globally, 20 million manufacturing jobs could be replaced by automated tools by 2030 (PatentPC)

Most of these automated tools are robots, not strictly AI, but some of these lost jobs will be replaced with new AI tools.

By 2030, 14% of employees will have been forced to change their career because of AI (McKinsey)

That's 14% of the global workforce, or 375 million workers. It's little wonder that AI courses to help workers upskill in the new technology are becoming more and more popular.

Wall Street expects to replace 200,000 roles with AI in the next 3 to 5 years (Bloomberg)

A 2025 Bloomberg Intelligence survey of 93 major banks including Citigroup, JPMorgan and Goldman Sachs found that workforces would be cut by an average of 3% by 2030 at the latest. Almost 1 in 4 executives expect reductions of 5 to 10%.

75% of CEOs think generative AI will significantly change their business within the next three years (PwC)

A large majority of business leaders polled by PwC foresaw the need for training in new skills, improving cybersecurity protocols, and a host of other changes — all due to the introduction and adoption of generative AI.

80% of the US workforce could have at least 10% of their tasks impacted by large language models (ARXIV)

Practically every job involves some tasks that are vulnerable to being automated by AI. Only a small minority of workers are totally unexposed to AI.

More than 7.5 million data entry jobs will be lost by 2027 (WEF)

This represents the largest predicted loss of jobs of any profession. The professions that are predicted to lose the most jobs are those extremely vulnerable to AI. Data entry clerks was first, administrative secretaries was second, and accounting was third.

41% of employers worldwide intend to reduce their workforce because of AI in the next five years (World Economic Forum)

The 2025 Future of Jobs report found that 92 million roles could be displaced by 2030, although it forecast a net gain of 78 million new jobs.

47% of US workers are at risk of losing their jobs to automation over the coming decade (CEPR)

In this case, automation also includes non-AI tools like robots.

It will take at least 20 years to automate just half of current worldwide work tasks (McKinsey)

While the potential economic gains from automation are great, they are a difficult potential to fully realize. Various barriers prevent widespread adoption of automation tools; these barriers, which can be legal, political, economic, social, technological, or something else entirely, may take decades to overcome.

AI's Current Impact on the Job Market

30% of US companies have replaced workers with AI tools like ChatGPT

According to a Resume Templates survey of nearly 1,000 US business leaders, 90% of companies have already adopted AI. This year, the amount of companies replacing workers with AI could rise to 38%.

From January to early June 2025, 77,999 tech job losses were directly linked to AI (Final Round AI)

Cuts at Amazon and Microsoft among others contributed to 491 people losing their jobs to AI every day.

40% of companies that are adopting AI are automating rather than augmenting human work (CNN)

That's according to the CEO of AI giant Anthropic, who also notes that the ratio is moving further toward automation.

Since 2000, automation has resulted in 1.7 million manufacturing jobs being lost (BuiltIn)

The introduction of automotive tools is also linked with increased competition, lower wages, and other negative effects beyond job loss.

13.7% of US workers report having lost their job to a robot (Socius)

Hundreds of thousands of workers have already been displaced by AI. Moreover, the displaced have, when surveyed, put forth much higher estimates of the share of the overall workforce that has likewise been displaced by a robot. They have put forth this figure: 46.9%. And this estimate has, on average, been put forth by those who have been displaced. Meanwhile, an average estimate put forth by individuals not displaced has been closer to 29%. Regardless of the side of the aisle from which one is coming, these figures are not even close to accurate.

Which Careers Are Exposed to AI?

Two-thirds of all jobs in the US and Europe are exposed to automation (Goldman Sachs)

That doesn't mean these jobs are all going to be fully automated. Exposure to automation just means that some of the tasks involved in a particular career can be automated.

40% of jobs worldwide are exposed to AI (IMF)

Hundreds of millions of people still lack access to the internet. As technology continues to spread around the world, the proportion of workers exposed to AI — and therefore to being automated — may well increase.

60% of jobs in advanced economies could be impacted by AI (IMF)

"Impacted" is a deliberately neutral term. According to the IMF's report, about half of those impacted by AI will be benefited. The other half will be negatively impacted. For example, their wages might decrease, or they could outright lose their job.

19% of workers are employed in the jobs most exposed to AI (Pew)

To calculate which jobs were most exposed to AI, researchers at Pew ranked professions based on how much workers relied on tasks that could be fully automated. The top 25% of jobs, when ranked this way, were considered "most exposed" to AI.

27% of workers with a bachelor's degree or higher are employed in jobs most exposed to AI (Pew)

Employees who were more educated were more likely to hold jobs considered highly exposed to AI. Only 3% of employees without a high school diploma worked in the kinds of jobs that are most exposed to AI. That figure went up to 12% for those with a high school diploma, 19% for those with some college, and 27% for workers who at least held a bachelor's degree.

Workers in jobs considered most exposed to AI earned $13.3/hr more than those in jobs least exposed to AI (Pew)

Better-paid jobs are currently more at risk of being lost to AI. While workers in the jobs most exposed to AI earned an average of $33.3 per hour, those employed in jobs least exposed to AI earned just $20 per hour on average.

Widespread adaptation of current automation tech could affect half of the world economy (McKinsey)

That represents some 1.2 billion employees and $14.6 trillion in wages. For context, $14.6 trillion is larger than the GDP of all countries bar China and the US, and is more than three times larger than the third-largest GDP.

AI Replacing Work Tasks

34% of all business-related tasks are already performed by machines (WEF)

The remaining 66% of tasks are performed by humans. This represents a minor but significant decrease in the share of tasks being performed entirely by non-humans. The researchers at the WEF suggest this could be due to the fact that AI and other automotive tools often help humans perform tasks more efficiently, rather than performing them independently.

Technology and machines play at least some role in 53% of work tasks (WEF)

The 2025 Future of Jobs report found that only 47% of work tasks are mainly performed by humans alone. 22% are done mainly by machines and algorithms, with the remainder being done by a combination of man and machine.

25% of all work tasks could be done by AI (Goldman Sachs)

Some professions entail a greater number of responsibilities that might be fully automated by artificial intelligence. For instance, 46% of the responsibilities handled by individuals in administrative jobs, and 44% of the tasks performed by legal professionals, could be completed by AI. In contrast, only 6% of the tasks associated with construction, and a mere 4% of the responsibilities tied to maintenance work, could be performed by AI.

19% of US workers could see more than half of their tasks impacted by AI (OpenAI)

In this case, "AI" refers specifically to systems that are equivalent to OpenAI's GPT-4.

Tasks that are highly exposed to AI are important in 77% of all jobs (Pew)

As things stand, AI is far better at some tasks than others. However, the tasks that it is great at, and therefore is most likely to automate, are important or extremely important in 77% of all jobs.

19% of US workers could have at least half of their tasks impacted by LLMs (ARXIV)

The number of workers who could see the majority of their job automated is relatively small at the minute. However, that 19% still represents hundreds of thousands of people — and will almost certainly grow as AI tools become more advanced.

Employers think 34% of tasks will be fully automated by 2030 (WEF)

That actually represents a significant decrease from 2023 predictions, when employers predicted that 42% of tasks would be wholly automated by 2027. This more conservative estimate could reflect doubts about whether AI tools will continue improving at the pace they have over the last few years.

65% of tasks related to data processing and information could be fully automated by 2027 (WEF)

These were the types of tasks most vulnerable to automation. In comparison, employers surveyed by the WEF predict that just 35% of tasks related to reasoning and decision-making could be automated by 2027.

Notable Jobs and Tasks AI Can't Replace

AI can only economically replace vision-based tasks accounting for just 0.4% of the total wages earned in the US (MIT)

According to a 2023 study by researchers at MIT, computer-vision AI can only automate tasks that account for just 1.6% of the wages earned by non-agricultural workers in the US. However, in most cases it would actually be more expensive to switch from humans to AI. Researchers estimated that it would be cheaper to replace just 23% of those wages that are automable.

23% of workers are in the jobs least exposed to AI (Pew)

The important tasks in these jobs were those resistant to automation. Take nannies, for example. The most important skills required to care for children are not particularly exposed to AI. That makes the job as a whole less exposed to AI than, for example, mechanical drafters.

40% of jobs in emerging markets are exposed to AI (IMF)

Emerging markets are usually less oriented toward services than established, high-income economies. Therefore, they contain fewer jobs that involve tasks that are automable by AI tools.

Just 26% of jobs in low-income countries are exposed to AI (IMF)

The vast majority of jobs in low-income countries involve tasks that are currently not automable by AI. In part, that's because significant proportions of workers in low-income countries still work in professions like subsistence agriculture. These roles are automable — just not by AI tools.

63% of business leaders surveyed by CEPR think AI won't affect employment rates in high-income countries (CEPR)

While 27% think AI will increase unemployment in high-income countries, most respondents were unsure about their answers.

Half of jobs will still be safe from full automation by 2045 (Goldman Sachs)

That being said, 60% of occupations could be impacted by AI as soon as 2030. These professions could see wage pressure as competition rises due to the automation of key tasks.

How People Are Responding to the Threat of AI Replacing Jobs

Over the next three years, 120 million workers will undergo retraining due to AI changing business demands (SEO.ai)

Training is one of the major barriers to the widespread adoption of AI tools. It represents a significant cost burden to any employer considering embracing AI. Nevertheless, tens of millions of workers will be retrained, either to use AI tools or to perform new tasks after old ones are automated by AI.

84% of employees worldwide are receiving significant organizational support to learn AI skills (McKinsey)

Employers who fail to train their workers in AI may find themselves falling behind their competitors. That could drive this statistic higher in coming years.

48% of US workers want more formal Gen AI training from their organization (McKinsey)

Training is the single biggest factor that would see more employees integrate AI into their daily work routines.

AI is the highest priority in the training strategies of companies with more than 50,000 employees (WEF)

Larger companies are more likely to embrace and fully adopt AI tools, which naturally means more of them will have to make AI training a top priority. Various industries also have AI as the highest priority of their training strategies, including IT services, media and entertainment, telecommunications, and electronics.

AI Causing Widespread Worry Among Workers

32% of US workers fear that AI will lead to fewer job opportunities (Pew)

All in all, 52% of workers are worried by AI, compared to just 36% who are hopeful. Only 29% feel excited, while 33% feel overwhelmed.

39% of workers are concerned they won't receive adequate training in new technology (PwC)

It's essential to keep pace with tech updates when you're trying to make it in a work world that is ever more competitive. Most of today's workers are concerned that they won't be trained to use tech that's current, much less tech that hasn't come out yet, such as new AI tools. This aligns with the findings of a recent PwC survey, which also found that employees who believe they have only a few skills that are in demand are much more likely to ask for raises or promotions, feel good about their jobs, and be willing to look for a new employer.

24% of workers fear that AI will make their job obsolete (SurveyMonkey / CNBC)

Those who are most concerned are younger workers, workers of color, and workers earning lower wages. The fact that lower-wage workers are more worried is interesting, considering the fact that other research shows that those earning higher wages are statistically more likely to be displaced.

43% of workers expect AI to cause their job to significantly change in the next five years (Survey Monkey)

This isn't necessarily bad. However, significant job changes often result in increased pressure and stress due to the need to adapt, especially if an employer does not provide retraining.

Just 32% of employees think their company has been transparent about its use of AI (Asana)

Perhaps unsurprisingly, workers are less likely to think this if they are lower down in the business hierarchy. While 44% of executives thought their company has been transparent about its AI usage, only 38% of managers agreed, and that figure fell to 25% among individual contributors.

55% of workers think AI will eliminate more jobs than it will create (BMG)

Despite reassurances from leaders in the AI space, people are still wary of this rapidly evolving technology. Just under half of respondents to the same poll said they thought it was likely that humans would eventually lose control of AI systems altogether.

US unemployment could reach 20% in the next five years (CNN)

That's the warning from the Anthropic CEO. It echoes fears that AI will not create as many jobs as it displaces.

Who is Most Worried About AI Replacing Their Job

81.6% of digital marketers think that content writers will lose jobs due to AI (SEO.ai)

Content production has been one of the industries most impacted by AI, so it's no surprise the vast majority of those involved in content creation predict jobs will be lost.

52% of people aged 18-24 are worried that AI will negatively impact their future careers (BMG)

Young workers have the most time ahead of them — time in which AI tools can become even more advanced, and pose even more of a challenge to human workers. For context, just 39% of all respondents in this poll indicated concern about their future career prospects being negatively impacted by AI.

Young workers are 129% more likely to be worried than older workers about AI making their job obsolete (SurveyMonkey)

Among workers aged 18-24, 32% said they were somewhat or very worried that AI would soon make their job obsolete. Up against that, only 14% of workers aged 65 and older reported feeling worried. Each to say younger workers in intermediate age groups seemed to harbor more and more worry about AI job loss, as you go down the age line.

38% of Asian workers are worried AI will make their job obsolete, compared to just 19% of white workers (SurveyMonkey)

Asian workers were the most worried, while white workers were the least afraid. In the middle, 32% of Black workers and 35% of Hispanic workers reported feeling concerned about AI making their job obsolete.

30% of workers earning under $50,000 per year are worried that AI will soon make their job obsolete (SurveyMonkey)

Interestingly, lower-income workers were almost twice as likely as higher earners to be worried about AI eliminating their jobs. Just 16% of workers earning over $150,000 reported feeling this stress.

Fully remote workers are 42% more likely than fully in-person employees to believe their job will be disrupted by AI (SurveyMonkey)

While 54% of fully remote workers think that their job will likely be changed by AI, only 38% of employees who work fully in-person think the same.

51% of workers in advertising and marketing believe their jobs will change due to AI (SurveyMonkey)

This represents one of the highest proportions of workers predicting job changes of any industry. AI tools are already being used by some companies to promote their products.

Where AI is Being Adopted

Companies with annual revenue of at least $500 million are adopting AI more quickly than smaller organizations (McKinsey)

Adopting AI comes with often significant costs. Larger organizations that can absorb these upfront expenses are thus more able and likely to adopt AI tools. According to the 2025 State of AI report, these larger companies tend to use AI in more areas of the business.

More than 75% of all organizations now use AI in at least one business function (McKinsey)

Larger companies are adapting more quickly, but AI adoption is already cutting across the majority of industries and businesses.

AI's Potential to Create New Careers

81% of office workers hold a generally favorable view of AI (SnapLogic)

AI might be taking some of their jobs, but office workers are still overwhelmingly positive about the new technology. More than four-fifths believe it improves their job performance and experience at work.

51% of office workers say AI lets them achieve better work-life balance (SnapLogic)

The utopian promise of AI, spread by major proponents like Elon Musk, is a world where work isn't necessary at all. For the minute, however, work remains one part of the work-life balance. A majority of workers are using AI to push the scale further toward "life."

Alternatively, just 6% of workers say AI will lead to more job opportunities in the long run (Pew)

31% predict the technology won't make much difference, while 32% think it will lead to job losses.

Among those using AI chatbots at work, 79% say it allows them to do things at least somewhat more quickly (Pew)

40% answered extremely/very. Only 29% said that AI chatbots had a similarly major positive impact on the quality of their work.

25.6% of organizations surveyed by the WEF expect AI to create jobs (WEF)

The business leaders polled by the WEF were quite divided over AI's potential impact, indicating the general uncertainty surrounding the ramifications of widespread AI adoption. A little under half of those surveyed believe it will create jobs, while a little under a quarter think it will eliminate jobs on balance. The degree of disagreement over AI's impact on jobs was higher than for any other change included in the poll.

Between 2023 and 2027, the profession with the largest net job growth worldwide will be "AI and Machine Learning Specialist" (WEF)

All of the professions that topped this ranking were new. That means there are few existing jobs to lose but many to gain, resulting in a huge net growth. The professions with the largest predicted raw growth in jobs were quite unexposed to AI: agricultural equipment operators, heavy truck and bus drivers, and so on. Each of these professions will likely add over two million jobs worldwide by 2027. For comparison, about one million "AI and Machine Learning Specialist" jobs are predicted to appear over the same timeframe.

Having access to an LLM resulted in 15% of employee tasks being completed faster with no loss in quality (ARXIV)

By allowing employees to complete more work in the same amount of time, AI tools might induce employers to cut back on workers.

Miscellaneous Stats About AI Replacing Jobs

17% of British workers think they can often or always tell when they are using an AI (ONS)

Workers are more likely to be confident they can spot an AI if they are male, younger, or with a degree.

26% of workers think they are considered lazy if they use AI (Asana)

While the vast majority of workers aren't worried about using AI tools, a significant proportion worry it could negatively impact how people view their work ethic. That's not an unreasonable concern, as being considered lazy could mean being passed up for a pay rise or promotion.

18% of workers feel like a fraud when they use AI for work (Asana)

Debates around the proper use of AI continue. The direction of popular culture will have a significant impact on this statistic. Will people accept the use of AI for work, or make it unacceptable?

15% of US workers are open to having an AI boss (Asana)

Americans are apparently more receptive to the idea of having a robot boss than British workers. Just 8% of workers in the UK said they'd be open to this idea.

One-third of all US jobs created in the last quarter-century didn't exist before (McKinsey)

Technically, these jobs either didn't exist or "barely existed." Technological advancements can eliminate jobs, but they often create entirely new professions that no one could have predicted.

Conclusion

AI is progressing so quickly that there is even disagreement among experts about the precise impact this emerging technology is likely to have on worldwide job numbers. AI might very well cause mass unemployment. But it's already enhancing the work lives of millions of workers. Conversely, hundreds of thousands of new jobs will be AI's gift to America. Yet, at the same time, millions of people are being displaced by robots. Nevertheless, as AI keeps moving ahead and being embraced, its effects on the world workforce — good or bad — will ramp up.

Resource

Josh Howarth (2025) Resource

https://explodingtopics.com/blog/ai-replacing-jobs

16.6 The age of the AI agent (Agentic Systems)

Introduction

We are entering an era where artificial intelligence (AI) agents are no longer mere tools but active, autonomous collaborators capable of reasoning, decision-making, and innovation. These AI agents can function independently, coordinate with other agents, and even supervise hybrid human-AI teams. This paper explores the evolving landscape of autonomous multiagent frameworks, hybrid teamwork, supervisor agents, advanced reasoning capabilities (levels 3 and 4), and evaluation (eval) agents that promise to transform research, workflows, and innovation itself.

Autonomous Multiagent Frameworks and Platforms for Workflows

The Rise of Multiagent Systems

Multiagent systems (MAS) consist of multiple interacting agents that work toward individual or shared goals. Each agent is autonomous, possessing its own perceptions, knowledge, and actions. In modern workflows, MAS can dynamically adapt to changes, optimize resource allocation, and enhance overall system resilience.

Platforms and Frameworks

Several frameworks now support the development of robust multiagent workflows:

- JADE (Java Agent DEvelopment Framework): A popular platform enabling distributed agent-based applications with standardized communication protocols.
- Microsoft Project Bonsai: Facilitates the design of AI agents using reinforcement learning and simulation-based training.
- OpenAI's ecosystem: Includes toolkits for developing agents capable of multimodal perception, code generation, and autonomous decision-making.

These platforms enable agents to manage supply chains, orchestrate clinical trials, perform financial modeling, and optimize industrial operations with minimal human intervention.

Hybrid Teams - The Human-AI Partnership

Hybrid teams blend human expertise with AI-driven efficiency. In such setups, AI agents handle routine tasks, data analysis, and pattern recognition, freeing humans to focus on creative and strategic decisions.

Examples and Benefits

- Healthcare: AI agents analyze patient data and suggest treatment options, while doctors make final clinical decisions.
- Scientific Research: AI proposes experiment designs or analyzes vast datasets, allowing scientists to focus on hypothesis formation and interpretation.
- Engineering and Design: AI generates multiple design prototypes, which human experts refine and validate.

These hybrid systems improve productivity, reduce errors, and foster new forms of innovation through symbiotic collaboration.

Supervisor Agents - Managing Complexity

As agent ecosystems grow in scale and complexity, supervisor agents emerge as critical orchestrators. These agents monitor the performance of other agents, manage conflicts, ensure compliance with overall system goals, and optimize resource usage.

Capabilities

- Policy enforcement: Supervisor agents ensure that individual agents adhere to operational or ethical constraints.
- Resource allocation: Dynamically distribute computational or physical resources across tasks.
- Performance evaluation: Monitor efficiency and suggest adjustments or retraining.

In essence, supervisor agents act as meta-managers, maintaining system integrity and coherence across highly distributed and complex tasks.

Reasoning Level 3 and 4 Agents - From Execution to Innovation

Traditional agents excel at executing predefined tasks (reasoning levels 1 and 2). However, reasoning level 3 and 4 agents go beyond to enable abstract reasoning, meta-reasoning, and even autonomous innovation.

Level 3: Abstract and Analogical Reasoning

At this level, agents can:

- Draw inferences from incomplete data.
- Use analogies to transfer knowledge from one domain to another.
- Plan complex, multi-step tasks without direct programming.

Level 4: Creative Reasoning and Discovery

Level 4 agents possess capabilities to:

- Formulate new hypotheses.
- Design novel experiments.
- Derive original scientific theories or engineering solutions.

Such agents mark a transition from reactive automation to proactive discovery, enabling breakthroughs in fields like drug development, materials science, and quantum computing.

Eval Agents

Continuous Self-Improvement

Eval agents specialize in monitoring, evaluating, and optimizing the performance of other agents or systems. They function as internal auditors and trainers within AI ecosystems.

Roles

- Performance Assessment: Evaluate task outcomes against defined metrics.
- Error Analysis: Identify failures and suggest corrective actions.
- Feedback Loop: Provide real-time insights for adaptive learning and system refinement.

Eval agents ensure that AI systems remain aligned with evolving objectives, maintain high reliability, and adapt effectively to new challenges.

Conclusion

The age of the AI agent signifies a profound shift in how we work, create, and innovate. Autonomous multiagent frameworks allow for scalable, adaptive workflows. Hybrid teams foster unprecedented synergy between humans and machines. Supervisor agents orchestrate complex systems, while advanced reasoning agents push the frontiers of autonomous research and discovery. Finally, eval agents maintain system integrity and drive continuous improvement.

Together, these advances not only augment human capability but also open new avenues for scientific exploration, societal problem-solving, and the creation of knowledge itself. The future belongs to those who can harness these intelligent agents to tackle the world's most complex challenges.

PART 6: OTHER EMERGING TECHNOLOGIES REQUIRING ADVANCED COMPUTE THAT WILL DISRUPT THE GLOBAL ECONOMY

Chapter 17: Other Technologies impacting the Global Economy

I. Introduction

A. Overview of emerging technologies and their potential economic impacts
B. Importance of understanding these technologies in the context of AGI and the future economy

A. Overview of Emerging Technologies and Their Potential Economic Impacts

The advent of emerging technologies such as Artificial General Intelligence (AGI), humanoid robotics, quantum computing, nanotechnology, extended reality (XR), and cryptocurrencies is reshaping the global economy in unprecedented ways. These innovations are not merely augmenting existing processes; they are fundamentally altering how industries operate, creating new economic paradigms, and transforming the nature of work itself. This chapter explores the potential economic impacts of these emerging technologies, emphasizing their interplay with AGI and the broader implications for future economic landscapes.

1. The Transformative Power of Emerging Technologies

Emerging technologies have the potential to drive significant productivity gains, foster innovation, and create entirely new markets. For instance, AGI promises to automate cognitive tasks across various sectors, leading to efficiency improvements and cost reductions. Similarly, humanoid robotics can perform manual labor in manufacturing, logistics, and even healthcare settings, augmenting human capabilities and addressing labor shortages.

Quantum Computing: One of the most disruptive technologies on the horizon, quantum computing offers the promise of exponentially faster data processing and problem-solving capabilities compared to classical computing. Industries such as finance, pharmaceuticals, and logistics could experience transformative impacts through enhanced data analysis, optimization of supply chains, and accelerated drug discovery processes. For example, quantum algorithms can solve complex optimization problems in logistics that would take classical computers an impractical amount of time, thereby significantly reducing operational costs.

Nanotechnology: This technology involves manipulating matter at the atomic and molecular levels, leading to innovations across diverse fields including medicine, materials science, and electronics. In healthcare, nanotechnology can lead to targeted drug delivery systems, significantly improving treatment efficacy and reducing side effects. The manufacturing sector may benefit from nanomaterials that enhance product durability and reduce weight, opening possibilities for new applications and energy efficiencies.

Extended Reality (XR): The combination of virtual reality (VR), augmented reality (AR), and mixed reality (MR) is creating immersive experiences that transform industries such as gaming, education, and training. XR technologies facilitate remote collaboration, skill development, and experiential learning, leading to more effective training programs that can be tailored to individual needs. For instance, XR can simulate real-world scenarios for medical professionals, enabling them to practice surgeries or emergency responses without risking patient safety.

Cryptocurrencies and Decentralized Finance (DeFi): Cryptocurrencies have emerged as a novel form of digital currency, disrupting traditional banking systems and introducing decentralized financial models. The implications for the economy are vast, as these technologies enable peer-to-peer transactions, reduce reliance on intermediaries, and create opportunities for financial inclusion in underserved populations. Moreover, DeFi platforms are innovating in lending, borrowing, and investment, challenging traditional financial institutions and prompting regulatory considerations.

2. Economic Impact Projections

The potential economic impacts of these emerging technologies are substantial. According to various estimates, AI alone could contribute over $15 trillion to the global economy by 2030. However, this growth does not come without challenges. As automation technologies evolve, significant workforce displacement is expected, particularly in sectors like manufacturing, transportation, and even professional services. For instance, autonomous vehicles threaten to disrupt the transportation industry, potentially displacing millions of driving jobs.

Furthermore, as humanoid robots and AI systems increasingly take over tasks traditionally performed by humans, there will be a pressing need for retraining and upskilling the workforce to adapt to these changes. A study by the World Economic Forum projects that while millions of jobs will be lost to automation, new roles will emerge that require distinctly human skills, such as creativity, empathy, and advanced problem-solving abilities.

3. The Interplay with AGI and Future Economic Landscapes

Understanding these technologies in the context of AGI is crucial for several reasons. First, AGI represents the pinnacle of AI development, with the potential to outperform humans across a broad range of cognitive tasks. As AGI systems evolve, they will likely integrate with other emerging technologies, amplifying their impacts on industries and job markets.

For example, in healthcare, the combination of AGI with nanotechnology could lead to groundbreaking innovations in personalized medicine, where treatment plans are tailored to individual genetic profiles, resulting in more effective therapies. In finance, AGI could revolutionize risk assessment, fraud detection, and trading strategies by processing vast amounts of data in real-time.

Furthermore, the rise of AGI raises ethical and governance questions that need to be addressed to harness its benefits while mitigating risks. As AGI systems begin to make decisions in critical areas such as healthcare, transportation, and law, there will be pressing concerns regarding accountability, transparency, and the potential for bias. Establishing regulatory frameworks and ethical guidelines will be essential to ensure that AGI technologies are developed and deployed responsibly.

4. Conclusion: The Importance of Understanding Emerging Technologies

In conclusion, the interplay between emerging technologies and AGI presents both challenges and opportunities for the global economy. As these technologies continue to evolve, understanding their potential economic impacts becomes imperative for policymakers, businesses, and individuals alike. Preparing for the disruptions they may cause, while also leveraging their transformative potential, will be key to fostering an inclusive and sustainable future economy.

Recognizing the need for collaboration between government, industry, and educational institutions will be crucial in addressing the workforce implications of these changes. As we stand on the brink of a new economic era defined by technological advancement, a proactive approach to understanding and managing these emerging technologies will be essential for navigating the complexities of the AGI-driven economy.

II. Humanoid Robotics

A. Definition and current state of humanoid robotics
1. Key players in the humanoid robotics industry
2. Recent advancements and prototypes

Humanoid Robotics

A. Definition and Current State of Humanoid Robotics

Humanoid robotics is a field within robotics focused on designing robots that resemble and mimic human appearance and behavior. These robots are engineered to perform tasks that require human-like dexterity, mobility, and cognitive capabilities. Unlike traditional industrial robots that operate in fixed environments, humanoid robots are built to interact with people and navigate complex environments autonomously. They have a diverse range of applications, from assisting in elderly care to participating in research and exploration missions, showcasing their potential to augment human capabilities and improve quality of life.

The development of humanoid robots involves multiple disciplines, including artificial intelligence, mechanical engineering, electronics, and cognitive science. Researchers and engineers strive to create robots that can walk, grasp objects, understand speech, and respond to social cues, making them more capable of engaging with humans in a natural way. This quest for human-like interaction involves not only replicating physical features but also developing advanced algorithms that enable robots to learn from their environments, adapt to new tasks, and understand human emotions and intentions.

1. Key Players in the Humanoid Robotics Industry

The humanoid robotics industry is dynamic and competitive, featuring a mix of established companies and innovative startups. Major players include:

Boston Dynamics: Known for its advanced robotic technologies, Boston Dynamics has developed several humanoid robots, including Atlas, a bipedal robot designed for a range of dynamic movements such as running, jumping, and navigating complex terrains. Their focus on mobility and agility has positioned them as leaders in the field.

SoftBank Robotics: The company is well-known for its humanoid robot, Pepper, which is designed to interact with people and provide assistance in various environments, such as retail and hospitality. Pepper's ability to recognize emotions and engage in conversations has made it a popular choice for customer service roles.

Honda: With its ASIMO robot, Honda has made significant strides in humanoid robotics. ASIMO is capable of walking, running, climbing stairs, and even recognizing faces and voices. Honda's emphasis on developing robots for practical use in daily life has led to collaborations in sectors like healthcare and education.

Toyota: Toyota has entered the humanoid robotics space with its T-HR3 robot, which showcases advanced control systems that allow for intuitive human-robot interaction. The T-HR3 is designed for various applications, including assisting with physical tasks in elder care and rehabilitation.

Agility Robotics: This company focuses on developing bipedal robots with advanced mobility features. Their robot, Cassie, is designed for research purposes and has gained attention for its ability to traverse diverse environments while maintaining stability and balance.

University Research Labs: Academic institutions worldwide contribute significantly to humanoid robotics research. For instance, the MIT Media Lab and the University of Tokyo's Intelligent Robotics Lab are renowned for their innovations in humanoid robotics, emphasizing both technological advancement and social implications.

2. Recent Advancements and Prototypes

The field of humanoid robotics has seen remarkable advancements in recent years, driven by breakthroughs in artificial intelligence, machine learning, and sensor technologies. Notable developments include:

Enhanced Mobility and Agility: Humanoid robots are becoming increasingly capable of dynamic movements. Boston Dynamics' Atlas has demonstrated impressive feats, such as backflips and parkour-like maneuvers, showcasing the potential for robots to navigate complex environments. Researchers are also developing robots that can walk on uneven surfaces, maintain balance during various activities, and adapt their movements based on real-time feedback.

Improved Human-Robot Interaction: Recent advancements in natural language processing and emotion recognition have led to robots that can understand and respond to human speech and emotions. SoftBank Robotics' Pepper utilizes AI algorithms to interpret human feelings and engage in empathetic conversations. Additionally, advancements in gesture recognition enable robots to respond to non-verbal cues, making interactions more intuitive.

Autonomous Navigation: The integration of advanced sensors, such as LiDAR and depth cameras, has enabled humanoid robots to navigate their environments with greater autonomy. These sensors provide real-time data about the surroundings, allowing robots to avoid obstacles and make decisions about their movements. For example, Honda's ASIMO can navigate through crowded spaces and adapt its path based on the location of humans.

Collaborative Robots (Cobots): A growing trend in humanoid robotics is the development of collaborative robots designed to work alongside humans. These robots are equipped with safety features and advanced sensing capabilities, allowing them to perform tasks in close proximity to people. Toyota's T-HR3 exemplifies this approach, designed to assist individuals in various settings without posing safety risks.

Research Prototypes: In addition to commercial applications, numerous research prototypes are being developed to explore the boundaries of humanoid robotics. For instance, the Sophia robot, developed by Hanson Robotics, has gained attention for its human-like appearance and conversational abilities. Sophia's design focuses on social interactions, making it a valuable tool for studying human-robot relationships and societal acceptance of robotics.

Integration with AI and Machine Learning: The convergence of humanoid robotics with AI technologies is paving the way for intelligent robots that can learn and adapt over time. Machine learning algorithms enable robots to improve their performance based on experience, allowing them to tackle increasingly complex tasks. This adaptability is crucial for applications in dynamic environments, such as healthcare, where robots may need to learn how to assist different patients.

Summary

The current state of humanoid robotics reflects a combination of advanced technologies, innovative designs, and a growing interest in human-robot collaboration. With key players pushing the boundaries of what is possible, the field continues to evolve rapidly, presenting exciting opportunities for the future. As humanoid robots become more capable of performing tasks traditionally reserved for humans, society will need to grapple with the implications of their integration into daily life, raising questions about ethics, labor, and the nature of human-robot relationships. As advancements continue, the potential for humanoid robots to enhance various sectors, from healthcare to entertainment, will redefine our understanding of work, assistance, and companionship in an increasingly automated world.

B. Economic implications

1. Impact on labor markets and job displacement
2. Potential for enhancing productivity and efficiency in various sectors

Economic Implications of Humanoid Robotics

B. Economic Implications

As humanoid robotics technology continues to advance, its economic implications become increasingly significant. These implications manifest in various forms, primarily through labor market transformations and the potential for enhanced productivity and efficiency across different sectors. While the emergence of humanoid robots poses challenges—such as job displacement, it also presents opportunities for economic growth and innovation. This section explores these dimensions in detail.

1. Impact on Labor Markets and Job Displacement

One of the most critical economic implications of humanoid robotics is their impact on labor markets. The integration of humanoid robots into various industries is likely to lead to significant changes in employment patterns. Job displacement is a primary concern, especially in sectors where routine tasks are prevalent. For instance, humanoid robots are increasingly being deployed in industries such as manufacturing, logistics, and customer service, where they can perform repetitive tasks with higher precision and efficiency than human workers.

Manufacturing and Warehousing: In manufacturing, humanoid robots can automate assembly line processes, leading to increased production rates and reduced labor costs. As companies adopt these technologies, there is a risk that low-skilled labor positions may be eliminated. For instance, in warehouses, robots can pick, pack, and sort goods with greater speed and accuracy than human workers. This shift may displace many jobs traditionally held by workers, particularly those in roles involving manual labor or routine operations.

Service Industries: The service sector is another area where humanoid robotics may lead to job displacement. Robots like SoftBank's Pepper are being used in customer-facing roles in retail and hospitality, performing tasks such as greeting customers, providing information, and processing transactions. While these robots enhance customer service experiences, they can also reduce the need for human employees in similar roles, particularly in environments where cost-cutting is a priority.

Cognitive Automation: Beyond physical tasks, humanoid robots are increasingly capable of cognitive functions, such as data analysis and decision-making. In sectors like finance and healthcare, AI-driven robots can analyze vast amounts of data to make informed recommendations or decisions. This development raises concerns about the displacement of jobs involving analysis and administrative functions, as organizations may prefer robots for their efficiency and accuracy.

Skill Gaps and Inequalities: The displacement of jobs due to humanoid robotics also raises concerns about skill gaps in the labor market. As certain roles become automated, workers may find themselves without the necessary skills to transition to new job opportunities. This situation could exacerbate existing inequalities, particularly for low-skilled workers who may have limited access to retraining and educational resources. Without effective interventions, the impact of job displacement could disproportionately affect marginalized communities, leading to higher rates of unemployment and economic hardship.

2. Potential for Enhancing Productivity and Efficiency in Various Sectors

Despite the challenges posed by job displacement, humanoid robotics hold significant potential for enhancing productivity and efficiency across various sectors. The ability of these robots to perform tasks with speed, precision, and consistency can lead to improved outcomes for businesses and economies as a whole.

Increased Production Efficiency: In manufacturing, humanoid robots can operate continuously without fatigue, enabling companies to increase production volumes and reduce downtime. Automation of repetitive tasks allows human workers to focus on more complex and value-added activities, ultimately driving innovation and competitiveness. As a result, organizations that adopt humanoid robotics may experience significant cost savings and improved profit margins.

Quality Improvement: Humanoid robots excel at performing tasks with a high degree of accuracy. In industries such as pharmaceuticals and electronics, where precision is crucial, the introduction of robots can lead to fewer defects and higher-quality products. By minimizing human error, businesses can enhance their reputation and customer satisfaction, further contributing to economic growth.

Data Processing and Analysis: The cognitive capabilities of humanoid robots enable them to process vast amounts of data quickly and effectively. In sectors like finance and healthcare, this can lead to improved decision-making and operational efficiency. For example, in healthcare, robots can analyze patient data to identify trends, predict outcomes, and optimize treatment plans. Such advancements not only improve the quality of care but can also reduce healthcare costs by streamlining processes and minimizing unnecessary interventions.

Collaborative Robots (Cobots): Humanoid robots can work alongside human workers in collaborative roles, enhancing productivity without replacing jobs. These collaborative robots, or "cobots," are designed to assist humans in tasks that require both human intuition and robotic precision. In warehouses, cobots can help human workers lift heavy items or automate repetitive tasks, improving overall efficiency and safety. This synergy allows companies to leverage the strengths of both humans and robots, creating a more productive work environment.

New Business Models and Innovation: The rise of humanoid robotics is also fostering the emergence of new business models and industries. Companies are exploring innovative applications for humanoid robots, from healthcare solutions that assist elderly patients to entertainment robots that provide companionship. This shift not only creates new job opportunities but also stimulates economic growth through the development of new markets and services.

Cost Savings and Economic Growth: By enhancing productivity and efficiency, humanoid robotics can lead to significant cost savings for businesses. These savings can be reinvested into research and development, employee training, and other initiatives that promote economic growth. Additionally, as companies grow and expand their operations, they can create new job opportunities in higher-skilled roles that focus on robotics maintenance, programming, and oversight.

Summary

The economic implications of humanoid robotics are complex and multifaceted. While the potential for job displacement poses significant challenges, the opportunities for enhanced productivity and efficiency cannot be overlooked. As businesses and industries adapt to the integration of humanoid robots, there will be a critical need for policies and programs that address the potential negative impacts on workers while also harnessing the benefits of increased automation. By embracing innovation and fostering a workforce that can thrive in an increasingly automated world, society can leverage the advantages of humanoid robotics to drive economic growth and improve quality of life. The path forward will require collaboration among stakeholders—governments, businesses, educational institutions, and workers—to create a sustainable economic framework that balances the benefits of technology with the need for social equity and workforce development.

C. Societal considerations

1. Human-robot interaction and acceptance
2. Ethical concerns and implications of humanoid robotics

Societal Considerations of Humanoid Robotics

C. Societal Considerations

As humanoid robotics technology continues to evolve and integrate into various aspects of society, it brings with it a host of societal considerations that must be carefully examined. This section explores two key dimensions: human-robot interaction and acceptance, and the ethical concerns and implications that arise with the deployment of humanoid robots. These factors will play a crucial role in shaping public perception, guiding policy decisions, and influencing the overall impact of humanoid robotics on society.

1. Human-Robot Interaction and Acceptance

The interaction between humans and humanoid robots is a central theme in understanding how these technologies will be integrated into everyday life. Successful human-robot interaction relies on factors such as usability, trust, and emotional connection. As humanoid robots become more sophisticated and capable, public acceptance will largely hinge on their ability to engage users in a natural and intuitive manner.

Usability and Design: The design of humanoid robots significantly impacts their acceptance. Robots that are easy to use, understand, and interact with are more likely to gain acceptance among users. Features such as responsive communication, user-friendly interfaces, and intuitive movement patterns contribute to a positive experience. For example, robots designed for healthcare settings, like robotic nursing assistants, must be user-friendly to ensure that both patients and healthcare workers feel comfortable and confident using them. If the technology appears cumbersome or unresponsive, it may foster resistance and skepticism.

Trust and Reliability: Trust is another crucial element in human-robot interaction. Users must feel confident in the robot's abilities and safety features. This is particularly important in high-stakes environments like healthcare and elderly care, where robots may be responsible for assisting vulnerable populations. Trust can be built through transparency in the robot's functions and clear communication of its capabilities and limitations. For instance, when robots provide care to the elderly, caregivers need to understand the decision-making processes of these machines to feel secure in their use.

Emotional Connection: Humanoid robots that exhibit human-like qualities—such as facial expressions, tone of voice, and social cues—may foster a stronger emotional connection with users. Robots designed for companionship, such as social robots for the elderly, can alleviate feelings of loneliness and isolation. However, the design must balance anthropomorphism and authenticity; overly human-like robots may create discomfort, known as the "uncanny valley" effect, where users feel uneasy due to the robot's almost-human appearance. Finding the right balance is essential for maximizing acceptance.

Cultural Factors: Cultural perspectives significantly influence how humanoid robots are received in society. Different cultures have varying attitudes towards technology, robots, and their roles in daily life. For instance, some cultures may embrace robots as valuable assistants and companions, while others may view them with skepticism or fear. Understanding these cultural nuances is essential for companies developing humanoid robots, as tailoring marketing strategies and public engagement efforts to align with cultural values can enhance acceptance.

2. Ethical Concerns and Implications of Humanoid Robotics

The deployment of humanoid robots raises a host of ethical concerns that must be addressed to ensure their responsible integration into society. These concerns encompass a wide range of issues, including labor rights, privacy, accountability, and the broader implications for human dignity and societal values.

Labor Rights and Job Displacement: One of the most pressing ethical concerns regarding humanoid robotics is the potential for job displacement. As robots take over tasks traditionally performed by humans, questions arise about the rights and responsibilities of companies and governments to protect displaced workers. There is a moral obligation to provide support for retraining and reskilling programs, as well as to create safety nets for those affected by automation. Policymakers must consider how to balance the economic benefits of robotics with the societal responsibility to ensure that all individuals can participate in the economy.

Privacy and Surveillance: Humanoid robots equipped with advanced sensors and data processing capabilities may collect vast amounts of personal data during their interactions with humans. This raises concerns about privacy and surveillance, especially in settings like homes, healthcare facilities, and public spaces.

Users must be informed about what data is being collected, how it will be used, and who has access to it. Establishing clear guidelines and ethical frameworks for data management is essential to protect individuals' privacy and maintain trust in humanoid robots.

Accountability and Responsibility: The question of accountability becomes increasingly complex as humanoid robots take on roles that require decision-making, particularly in critical sectors like healthcare and law enforcement. If a robot makes a mistake or causes harm, determining liability—whether it lies with the manufacturer, programmer, or the robot itself—becomes challenging. Ethical frameworks must be established to address these issues and provide clear guidelines for accountability. This includes developing standards for robot behavior, decision-making transparency, and mechanisms for addressing grievances.

Human Dignity and Autonomy: The introduction of humanoid robots into intimate and personal aspects of life raises ethical questions about human dignity and autonomy. For instance, robots designed to provide companionship or care may inadvertently affect the dynamics of human relationships and emotional well-being. The presence of humanoid robots in caregiving roles must be carefully managed to ensure that they complement human care rather than replace it. Moreover, ethical considerations should prioritize the autonomy and agency of individuals in their interactions with robots, allowing for human choice and preference in these relationships.

Social Implications and Human Value: Finally, the integration of humanoid robotics into society prompts a broader philosophical discussion about what it means to be human in a world increasingly shared with machines. As robots take on more human-like roles, society must grapple with questions about the value of human work, relationships, and creativity. It is essential to cultivate a societal narrative that recognizes the unique qualities of human experience, such as empathy, creativity, and critical thinking—while acknowledging the benefits that humanoid robots can provide.

Conclusion

The societal considerations surrounding humanoid robotics are vast and multifaceted. Understanding human-robot interaction and acceptance, alongside addressing ethical concerns, will be crucial for the successful integration of these technologies into society. As humanoid robots continue to evolve and become more prevalent, stakeholders must engage in ongoing dialogue to shape policies, standards, and frameworks that promote positive outcomes while mitigating risks. By prioritizing user experience, ethical considerations, and cultural sensitivities, society can harness the potential of humanoid robotics to enhance well-being and foster a future where technology complements the human experience. Ultimately, the responsible development and deployment of humanoid robots will depend on a collaborative approach that includes voices from diverse sectors of society, ensuring that the benefits of this technology are realized while upholding core human values.

III. Quantum Computers

A. Understanding quantum computing

1. Key principles of quantum mechanics as applied to computing
2. Comparison with classical computers

Quantum computing represents a paradigm shift in computational technology, harnessing the principles of quantum mechanics to solve complex problems more efficiently than classical computers. This section delves into the key principles underlying quantum computing and compares them with classical computing, illuminating the profound implications of this emerging technology.

A. Understanding Quantum Computing

1. Key Principles of Quantum Mechanics as Applied to Computing

At the heart of quantum computing lie several fundamental principles of quantum mechanics that enable the unique capabilities of quantum systems. These principles include superposition, entanglement, and quantum interference, all of which contribute to the enhanced processing power of quantum computers.

Superposition: In classical computing, data is represented in binary form, using bits that can exist in one of two states: 0 or 1. Quantum computing, however, utilizes quantum bits or qubits, which can exist simultaneously in multiple states due to the principle of superposition. A qubit can represent both 0 and 1 at the same time, enabling a quantum computer to process a vast amount of information concurrently. This characteristic allows quantum computers to perform complex calculations more efficiently than classical computers, as they can explore multiple solutions simultaneously.

Entanglement: Entanglement is a quantum phenomenon in which two or more qubits become correlated in such a way that the state of one qubit cannot be described independently of the others, regardless of the distance separating them. This interdependence allows for instantaneous information transfer between entangled qubits. In quantum computing, entanglement is harnessed to create powerful connections between qubits, enabling complex operations and computations that are not possible with classical systems.

The manipulation of entangled qubits can lead to faster problem-solving capabilities, making quantum computers particularly effective for tasks such as optimization, cryptography, and simulations of quantum systems.

Quantum Interference: Quantum interference refers to the phenomenon where the probability amplitudes of quantum states combine, leading to constructive or destructive interference. This principle is crucial in quantum algorithms, as it allows for the amplification of correct solutions and the cancellation of incorrect ones. Quantum algorithms, such as Grover's algorithm for unstructured search or Shor's algorithm for factoring large numbers, leverage interference to enhance the probability of arriving at the correct answer, significantly outperforming classical algorithms for specific tasks.

Together, these principles create a computational framework that differs fundamentally from classical computing. Quantum computers operate on a different mathematical model, utilizing linear algebra and complex probability amplitudes, leading to new algorithms and problem-solving techniques that have the potential to revolutionize fields such as cryptography, materials science, and artificial intelligence.

2. Comparison with Classical Computers

The distinctions between quantum computers and classical computers are stark and highlight the transformative potential of quantum technology. While both types of computers process information, they do so in fundamentally different ways, which impacts their capabilities, performance, and applications.

Processing Power: Classical computers utilize bits, which can represent a single binary state at any given time. Consequently, the processing power of classical computers scales linearly with the number of bits. In contrast, quantum computers utilize qubits, which can represent multiple states simultaneously due to superposition. As a result, the processing power of quantum computers scales exponentially with the number of qubits. This inherent parallelism allows quantum computers to solve complex problems much faster than classical computers, particularly in areas such as cryptography, optimization, and quantum simulations.

Algorithm Efficiency: Classical algorithms are limited by the constraints of classical computing architecture, which often leads to exponential time complexity for certain problems. Quantum algorithms, on the other hand, can exploit superposition and entanglement to provide significant speedups. For example, Shor's algorithm, which can factor large integers in polynomial time, poses a significant threat to classical encryption methods based on the difficulty of factoring.

Similarly, Grover's algorithm offers a quadratic speedup for unstructured search problems, illustrating how quantum computing can outperform classical methods for specific tasks.

Error Rates and Noise: Quantum computers are inherently susceptible to errors due to decoherence and noise, which arise from interactions with the environment. Qubits are delicate and can lose their quantum state quickly, leading to computational errors. Error correction in quantum computing is an active area of research, and while techniques such as quantum error correction codes have been developed, they introduce additional complexity to quantum algorithms. In contrast, classical computers are generally more stable and robust, making them less prone to errors. However, as quantum technology matures, improvements in error correction and qubit stability are expected to enhance the reliability of quantum systems.

Applications: The applications of classical and quantum computing differ significantly due to their underlying principles. Classical computers excel in tasks that require linear processing, such as word processing, spreadsheet calculations, and simple data analysis. However, as the complexity of tasks increases, particularly in fields such as cryptography, optimization, and simulation of quantum systems, classical computers face limitations. Quantum computers, with their ability to handle complex problem spaces, hold promise for applications in drug discovery, financial modeling, optimization problems, and machine learning. Industries that rely on large-scale data processing, like logistics, finance, and pharmaceuticals, stand to benefit from quantum advancements.

Energy Efficiency: Quantum computers have the potential to be more energy-efficient than classical computers for certain tasks. While classical computers require significant energy resources for computation, quantum systems can solve complex problems with fewer resources by leveraging quantum parallelism. However, the energy efficiency of quantum computing is still an area of active research, and practical implementations must address power consumption challenges associated with maintaining qubit coherence and operational environments.

Summary

Quantum computing represents a revolutionary advancement in technology, rooted in the principles of quantum mechanics that enable unprecedented processing power and efficiency. By leveraging superposition, entanglement, and quantum interference, quantum computers can outperform classical computers for specific tasks, with significant implications for industries ranging from cryptography to materials science. Understanding these foundational concepts is crucial for grasping the potential of quantum computing and its transformative impact on the future of technology and society. As research and development in quantum technology progress, the landscape of computing will continue to evolve, shaping new possibilities for innovation and problem-solving in the years to come.

B. Economic applications and implications

1. Breakthroughs in fields like cryptography, optimization, and drug discovery
2. Potential impact on industries such as finance, healthcare, and logistics

B. Economic Applications and Implications of Quantum Computing

Quantum computing is not just a theoretical advancement; it represents a significant shift in computational capabilities with profound economic applications and implications. As this technology matures, its potential to revolutionize various industries becomes increasingly apparent. This section delves into the breakthroughs facilitated by quantum computing in fields such as cryptography, optimization, and drug discovery, and explores its potential impacts on key sectors like finance, healthcare, and logistics.

1. Breakthroughs in Fields Like Cryptography, Optimization, and Drug Discovery

Cryptography

One of the most widely discussed applications of quantum computing is in the field of cryptography. Traditional cryptographic methods rely on mathematical problems that are computationally difficult for classical computers to solve. For example, RSA encryption, which secures a vast majority of online communications, is based on the difficulty of factoring large prime numbers. However, quantum computers, particularly with algorithms like Shor's algorithm, could factor these large numbers in polynomial time, effectively rendering classical encryption methods vulnerable.

This impending disruption is prompting researchers and industries to develop quantum-resistant encryption algorithms. These new algorithms are designed to secure data against the potential threats posed by quantum computing. The transition to quantum-resistant cryptography will have significant economic implications as organizations will need to invest in updating their security infrastructure. This includes financial institutions, government agencies, and businesses that rely on data integrity and confidentiality, creating a burgeoning market for quantum-safe solutions.

Optimization

Optimization problems are pervasive across industries, from logistics and supply chain management to financial portfolio optimization and manufacturing processes. Classical algorithms often struggle with complex optimization problems that involve numerous variables and constraints, leading to solutions that may be suboptimal or computationally prohibitive.

Quantum computing offers a new paradigm for addressing these challenges through quantum optimization algorithms, such as the Quantum Approximate Optimization Algorithm (QAOA) and Grover's search algorithm. These algorithms exploit quantum superposition and entanglement to explore multiple solutions simultaneously, enabling faster convergence on optimal solutions.

In logistics, for instance, quantum optimization could drastically improve route planning for delivery vehicles, reducing fuel consumption and improving delivery times. In finance, asset managers could utilize quantum computing to optimize investment portfolios under complex risk-return profiles. The economic impact of enhanced optimization capabilities could result in significant cost savings and increased efficiency across various sectors, enhancing overall productivity and competitiveness.

Drug Discovery

The pharmaceutical industry faces considerable challenges in drug discovery, including the lengthy and expensive processes of molecular modeling and simulation. Traditional computational methods often fall short in accurately predicting molecular interactions and behaviors, leading to high rates of failure in clinical trials.

Quantum computing has the potential to revolutionize drug discovery by simulating molecular structures and interactions at unprecedented scales. Quantum computers can model the quantum states of molecules, allowing researchers to identify potential drug candidates more efficiently. Algorithms such as the Variational Quantum Eigensolver (VQE) are already being developed to solve complex molecular problems, paving the way for faster and more accurate predictions.

The economic implications of accelerated drug discovery are vast. By reducing the time and cost associated with bringing new drugs to market, quantum computing could lead to lower healthcare costs and improved patient outcomes. Additionally, it could enable pharmaceutical companies to explore a wider range of therapeutic targets, potentially resulting in breakthroughs for diseases that currently have limited treatment options.

2. Potential Impact on Industries Such as Finance, Healthcare, and Logistics

Finance

The financial services industry is poised to be one of the most significantly impacted sectors by quantum computing. Beyond optimization in portfolio management, quantum computing could enhance risk analysis, fraud detection, and complex financial modeling. Traditional models often rely on simplifying assumptions that may not accurately reflect the complexities of real-world financial systems. Quantum computers could enable more nuanced models that better capture the dynamics of financial markets.

Moreover, quantum computing can facilitate faster transaction processing and improve the efficiency of blockchain technologies. As quantum algorithms advance, they could enhance the speed and security of transactions, leading to more robust financial systems. However, the potential risks posed by quantum computing to current encryption standards necessitate swift adaptation in security protocols, driving demand for new quantum-safe technologies within the financial sector.

Healthcare

In addition to its role in drug discovery, quantum computing could transform healthcare through improved diagnostics and personalized medicine. By analyzing vast datasets more efficiently, quantum algorithms could identify patterns in patient data that are currently undetectable using classical methods. This capability could lead to earlier diagnosis of diseases and more effective treatment plans tailored to individual patient profiles.

Furthermore, quantum computing could enhance medical imaging techniques, allowing for faster and more accurate interpretations of complex imaging data. The economic implications of these advancements could lead to a reduction in healthcare costs and improved patient outcomes, resulting in a more efficient healthcare system.

Logistics

The logistics and transportation industry stands to benefit immensely from the optimization capabilities of quantum computing. As global supply chains become increasingly complex, the need for efficient routing, inventory management, and demand forecasting grows. Quantum computing can address these challenges by enabling more sophisticated modeling of supply chain dynamics.

For instance, quantum algorithms could optimize delivery routes in real-time, taking into account traffic patterns, weather conditions, and other variables that affect delivery times. This optimization could lead to reduced operational costs and improved customer satisfaction. Moreover, quantum computing could enhance warehouse management through better inventory forecasting, minimizing stockouts and excess inventory.

The implications of these improvements extend beyond individual companies to the broader economy. By enhancing the efficiency of logistics and supply chains, quantum computing could drive down costs across various industries, leading to lower prices for consumers and increased competitiveness for businesses.

Summary

The economic applications of quantum computing are poised to transform a variety of industries, with breakthroughs in cryptography, optimization, and drug discovery leading the charge. The potential impact on finance, healthcare, and logistics underscores the profound implications of this technology for the global economy. As organizations adapt to harness the capabilities of quantum computing, significant investment will be required to ensure security, develop new algorithms, and retrain the workforce. Ultimately, the successful integration of quantum computing into existing economic frameworks has the potential to create new markets, drive innovation, and improve efficiencies across numerous sectors, marking a pivotal moment in technological advancement.

C. Challenges and limitations

1. Technical hurdles in scaling quantum computers
2. Ethical considerations regarding access and misuse

C. Challenges and Limitations of Quantum Computing

Quantum computing represents a profound shift in computational capabilities, promising to solve problems that are intractable for classical computers. However, as the field continues to evolve, it faces a myriad of challenges and limitations that could hinder its widespread adoption and effectiveness. This section delves into two primary categories of challenges: technical hurdles in scaling quantum computers and ethical considerations regarding access and potential misuse.

1. Technical Hurdles in Scaling Quantum Computers

A. Quantum Decoherence

One of the most significant technical challenges in developing quantum computers is the issue of quantum decoherence. Quantum bits, or qubits, are the fundamental units of quantum information. Unlike classical bits, which can be in one of two states (0 or 1), qubits can exist in superpositions of states, allowing them to perform many calculations simultaneously. However, this unique property is extremely sensitive to environmental disturbances, such as temperature fluctuations and electromagnetic radiation, which can cause qubits to lose their quantum state. This phenomenon, known as decoherence, effectively limits the time available for quantum computations.

To mitigate decoherence, researchers are exploring various techniques, including error correction codes and improved isolation of qubits from their environment. However, these solutions often require additional qubits and complex architectures, complicating the design of scalable quantum systems. The challenge lies in developing robust qubit technologies that can maintain coherence long enough to perform useful computations without excessive error rates.

B. Qubit Fidelity and Error Rates

Closely related to decoherence is the issue of qubit fidelity, which refers to the accuracy with which qubits can be manipulated and measured. High fidelity is essential for reliable quantum computation, as even small errors can compound quickly due to the entangled nature of quantum states. Current qubit technologies, including superconducting qubits, trapped ions, and topological qubits, each have their own limitations in terms of fidelity and scalability.

For instance, superconducting qubits can achieve relatively high fidelity but often suffer from increased noise levels at larger scales, making it challenging to maintain coherence across many qubits. Meanwhile, trapped ions offer high fidelity and longer coherence times but face difficulties in scaling due to the complexity of trapping and manipulating large numbers of ions simultaneously.

To overcome these hurdles, researchers are developing new qubit designs and architectures, such as quantum error correction codes and fault-tolerant quantum computing, which aim to protect quantum information from errors. However, implementing these solutions adds significant overhead and complexity to the quantum systems, making scalability a persistent challenge.

C. Resource Requirements and Cost

Scaling quantum computers also requires substantial resources in terms of power, space, and funding. Current quantum computing technologies necessitate sophisticated cryogenic cooling systems to maintain qubit temperatures close to absolute zero, along with complex control systems for qubit manipulation and measurement. These requirements impose significant challenges for scaling quantum systems to larger numbers of qubits.

Moreover, the financial investment needed to build and operate quantum computers is substantial. Many companies and research institutions are investing billions of dollars into quantum research and development, yet the path to achieving practical, large-scale quantum computers remains uncertain. As such, the high cost and resource demands pose barriers to widespread adoption and commercialization of quantum technologies.

2. Ethical Considerations Regarding Access and Misuse

A. Digital Divide and Access to Quantum Technology

As quantum computing technology advances, there is a pressing concern regarding access and equity. The benefits of quantum computing are likely to accrue primarily to those who can afford to invest in and utilize these technologies, potentially exacerbating existing inequalities in society. Organizations with substantial resources, such as large corporations and government agencies, may gain significant competitive advantages over smaller enterprises, startups, and less affluent nations.

This digital divide poses ethical dilemmas regarding equitable access to quantum technologies. If quantum computing is primarily available to a select few, it could hinder innovation and economic opportunities for broader populations. Policymakers and industry leaders must consider strategies to democratize access to quantum computing, ensuring that its benefits are distributed fairly and inclusively across various sectors and communities.

B. Misuse of Quantum Computing

The potential misuse of quantum computing capabilities raises serious ethical concerns, particularly in areas such as cybersecurity, privacy, and surveillance. As discussed earlier, quantum computers could effectively break many current encryption protocols, rendering sensitive data vulnerable to malicious actors. This capability poses significant risks to personal privacy, corporate security, and national defense.

For instance, if adversarial states or criminal organizations gain access to quantum computing technology, they could exploit it for nefarious purposes, such as hacking into secure communications, stealing proprietary information, or disrupting critical infrastructure. The implications of such misuse underscore the need for robust regulatory frameworks to govern the development and deployment of quantum technologies.

Moreover, ethical considerations must also extend to the broader societal impacts of quantum computing. As quantum systems become more integrated into various sectors, the potential for misuse could lead to increased surveillance and control over individuals, raising questions about privacy rights and civil liberties. It is essential for stakeholders to address these ethical concerns proactively, ensuring that the development of quantum technologies aligns with societal values and respects individual rights.

C. Regulatory and Governance Challenges

The rapidly evolving landscape of quantum computing presents challenges for regulatory bodies tasked with overseeing its development and application. Current legal frameworks may be ill-equipped to address the unique characteristics of quantum technologies, necessitating the creation of new policies and regulations that adequately reflect their complexities and implications.

Governments and international organizations will need to collaborate to establish standards and guidelines for the ethical use of quantum computing, particularly in sensitive areas like security, healthcare, and finance. These regulations should prioritize transparency, accountability, and fairness in the deployment of quantum technologies, ensuring that they are used responsibly and ethically.

Furthermore, the global nature of quantum research and development complicates governance efforts, as different countries may have varying approaches to regulation and ethical considerations. International cooperation will be essential to address the challenges posed by quantum computing and to establish a coherent framework that promotes responsible innovation while mitigating risks.

D. Quantum-Powered AI and its Disruptive Impact on the Global Economy: Utopia or Dystopia?

Introduction

The convergence of quantum computing and artificial intelligence (AI) represents a paradigm shift with profound implications for the global economy. With major players like Google and Microsoft developing cutting-edge quantum-powered AI chips—such as Google's Willow chip and Microsoft's AI-optimized hardware—the potential for accelerating AI capabilities to unprecedented levels is now within reach. This paper explores how quantum-powered AI can lead to both a utopian and dystopian future if left unchecked, with significant consequences for economic structures, labor markets, global governance, and societal stability.

The Rise of Quantum-Powered AI

Quantum computing, leveraging the principles of superposition and entanglement, has the potential to exponentially increase computational power. AI models, which currently rely on classical computing, face bottlenecks due to energy consumption and processing speed. The advent of quantum AI chips like Google's Willow and Microsoft's quantum-optimized AI processors promise to eliminate these barriers. These chips are designed to accelerate machine learning algorithms, optimize complex decision-making processes, and provide solutions to problems previously deemed computationally intractable.

Technological Capabilities

1. Enhanced Machine Learning: Quantum AI chips can analyze vast datasets at speeds classical AI cannot match.
2. Optimization Problems: Applications in supply chain logistics, financial modeling, and drug discovery will be revolutionized.

3. Cryptographic Advancements: Quantum computing can crack existing encryption protocols while also enabling quantum-secure communication.
4. Material Science & Drug Discovery: Quantum-powered simulations could lead to breakthroughs in pharmaceuticals and clean energy.

Utopian Scenario: The Quantum AI Renaissance

If quantum-powered AI is harnessed responsibly, it could usher in an era of technological and economic prosperity.

Economic Growth & Productivity

- Automation Efficiency: Quantum AI could optimize industrial automation, reducing waste and improving manufacturing efficiency.
- New Industries & Job Creation: Just as the internet created a new digital economy, quantum AI could spur the development of new industries such as quantum cybersecurity, AI ethics consulting, and bioinformatics.
- Financial Forecasting: Quantum-enhanced AI could allow for near-perfect economic modeling, reducing financial risks and stabilizing global markets.

Healthcare & Scientific Advancements

- Medical Breakthroughs: Quantum-powered AI could expedite the development of personalized medicine, optimize complex biological simulations, and lead to cures for previously untreatable diseases.
- Climate Change Mitigation: Quantum AI could revolutionize energy storage, optimize renewable energy grids, and improve carbon capture techniques.

Global Equity and Governance

- Economic Democratization: If widely accessible, quantum-powered AI could bridge the economic gap between developed and developing nations.
- Enhanced Decision-Making: Governments could use quantum AI to create more informed policies and optimize social welfare programs.

Dystopian Scenario: The Perils of Unchecked Quantum AI

While quantum-powered AI holds incredible promise, if left unchecked, it could lead to economic upheaval and geopolitical instability.

Mass Unemployment & Wealth Disparity

- Job Displacement: The integration of quantum AI in finance, healthcare, and manufacturing could lead to mass unemployment, particularly for white-collar and skilled labor sectors.
- Economic Polarization: Wealth could become concentrated among corporations and nations with access to quantum AI, exacerbating social inequalities.

Cybersecurity & AI Warfare

- Encryption Collapse: Quantum AI's ability to break classical cryptographic systems could lead to data breaches at an unprecedented scale.
- Autonomous Weaponization: Nations with quantum AI-driven military systems could gain an unparalleled strategic advantage, leading to new arms races and conflicts.

Corporate and Government Overreach

- Surveillance State: Quantum AI could enable hyper-surveillance, eroding privacy and civil liberties.
- Monopolization: Companies controlling quantum AI infrastructure could dictate market trends, stifling competition and innovation.

Regulatory & Ethical Considerations

To navigate between these two extremes, global regulatory frameworks are needed.

- International AI Governance: Collaboration between governments, tech corporations, and research institutions is necessary to establish ethical standards.
- Quantum AI Ethics Boards: Independent regulatory bodies should oversee the responsible development of quantum AI.
- Equitable Access Initiatives: Ensuring global accessibility of quantum AI will prevent monopolization and economic disparity.

Summary

Quantum-powered AI, exemplified by innovations such as Google's Willow chip and Microsoft's AI-driven quantum processor, has the potential to transform the global economy for better or worse. If responsibly managed, it could lead to a utopian technological renaissance, enhancing productivity, innovation, and equity. However, if left unchecked, it could exacerbate global inequalities, displace jobs, and introduce new security threats. Careful governance, ethical considerations, and proactive policymaking will be essential in shaping the future of quantum AI and ensuring that it benefits all of humanity

Conclusion

While quantum computing holds immense promises for transforming various industries and solving complex problems, it faces significant challenges and limitations. Technical hurdles such as decoherence, qubit fidelity, and resource requirements pose obstacles to scaling quantum systems effectively. Additionally, ethical considerations regarding access and potential misuse highlight the need for thoughtful approaches to governance and regulation in this rapidly evolving field. As stakeholders navigate these challenges, it will be crucial to ensure that the benefits of quantum computing are accessible to all and that its development aligns with societal values and ethical principles. By addressing these challenges proactively, the quantum computing community can help shape a future where this transformative technology is harnessed responsibly and effectively for the greater good.

IV. Nanotechnology

A. Definition and scope of nanotechnology

1. Applications in various fields (medicine, materials science, electronics)
2. Current research and future possibilities

A. Definition and Scope of Nanotechnology

Nanotechnology refers to the manipulation and control of matter at the nanoscale, typically between 1 to 100 nanometers (nm). To put that in perspective, a nanometer is one-billionth of a meter, far smaller than the diameter of a human hair, which is roughly 80,000 to 100,000 nm. At this scale, materials and structures can exhibit unique physical, chemical, and biological properties that differ significantly from their macroscopic counterparts. These properties are due to the increased relative surface area and quantum effects that become significant at the nanoscale.

Nanotechnology has become a multidisciplinary field, drawing from physics, chemistry, biology, materials science, and engineering to develop new technologies and applications. The scope of nanotechnology is vast and includes fields as diverse as medicine, electronics, energy, environmental science, and materials development. Nanotechnology's ability to work at the molecular and atomic level enables scientists and engineers to design new materials and devices with properties tailored for specific functions, opening doors to previously unimaginable innovations.

1. Applications in Various Fields

A. Medicine and Healthcare

One of the most exciting and impactful areas of nanotechnology is in medicine, where it holds the promise of revolutionizing diagnosis, treatment, and prevention of diseases. Nanomedicine involves the use of nanomaterials, nanoparticles, and nanoscale tools for medical applications, providing new ways to target diseases at the cellular and molecular levels. This can lead to more effective treatments with fewer side effects. For example:

- Drug Delivery: Nanoparticles can be engineered to deliver drugs directly to diseased cells, minimizing damage to healthy cells and reducing the side effects of treatments like chemotherapy. These nanocarriers can be designed to release drugs in response to specific biological triggers, such as the acidic environment of a tumor or the presence of certain enzymes.
- Diagnostics: Nanotechnology enables the development of highly sensitive diagnostic tools. Quantum dots, for instance, are nanoscale semiconductor particles that can be used to detect specific biomarkers associated with diseases, such as cancer or infectious agents. These tools allow for earlier detection of diseases, often before symptoms appear, which can improve outcomes.
- Regenerative Medicine: Nanotechnology is also playing a significant role in tissue engineering and regenerative medicine. Nanomaterials can be used to create scaffolds that mimic the extracellular matrix of tissues, promoting the growth of new cells and facilitating the repair of damaged tissues. Nanotechnology could lead to breakthroughs in healing injuries, growing organs, and treating degenerative diseases.

B. Materials Science

Nanotechnology is transforming materials science by allowing scientists to develop materials with unprecedented properties. These materials can be lighter, stronger, more conductive, or more resistant to wear and corrosion than traditional materials. The ability to manipulate the structure of materials at the nanoscale opens up a range of possibilities:

- Carbon Nanotubes (CNTs): These are cylindrical molecules made of carbon atoms arranged in a hexagonal pattern. CNTs are incredibly strong (about 100 times stronger than steel), lightweight, and have excellent electrical conductivity. They are used in various applications, from electronics to structural materials in aerospace and automotive industries.
- Graphene: Another revolutionary nanomaterial, graphene, consists of a single layer of carbon atoms arranged in a two-dimensional honeycomb lattice. It has remarkable

properties, including high electrical and thermal conductivity, mechanical strength, and flexibility. Graphene is being explored for use in flexible electronics, energy storage (batteries and supercapacitors), and even in desalination technologies.

- Nano-coatings: Nanotechnology enables the development of coatings that can impart new properties to surfaces. For example, self-cleaning coatings, often inspired by the lotus leaf, can repel water and prevent the accumulation of dirt and debris. Anti-corrosion coatings, thermal barriers, and antimicrobial surfaces are other applications of nano-coatings.

C. Electronics and Computing

Nanotechnology is driving significant advancements in the field of electronics, where the trend towards miniaturization has led to the development of smaller, faster, and more efficient devices. As traditional silicon-based transistors reach their physical limits in terms of size and performance, nanotechnology offers new solutions to continue the progress in computing power and electronic devices.

- Nanoscale Transistors: The development of transistors at the nanoscale is critical to sustaining Moore's Law, which predicts the doubling of transistors on a chip every two years. Nanoscale transistors, using materials like carbon nanotubes or semiconductor nanowires, allow for more compact and powerful processors.
- Quantum Dots in Displays: Nanotechnology has enabled the creation of quantum dots, which are semiconductor nanoparticles that can be used in displays to produce more vibrant colors with lower energy consumption. Quantum dot technology is being incorporated into high-definition televisions, monitors, and mobile device screens.
- Flexible Electronics: Nanotechnology allows for the development of flexible, stretchable, and wearable electronic devices. These devices, often incorporating nanomaterials like graphene or silver nanowires, could lead to new applications in areas such as healthcare monitoring, environmental sensing, and smart textiles.

D. Energy

Nanotechnology has the potential to address some of the most pressing energy challenges by improving the efficiency of energy production, storage, and consumption.

- Solar Cells: Nanotechnology is being used to improve the efficiency of photovoltaic cells, which convert sunlight into electricity. Nanomaterials like quantum dots and nanowires can be incorporated into solar cells to enhance light absorption and reduce energy losses, leading to more efficient solar panels.

- Energy Storage: Nanotechnology is also improving energy storage technologies, such as batteries and supercapacitors. By using nanostructured materials, it is possible to increase the surface area available for chemical reactions, leading to batteries with higher energy densities, faster charging times, and longer lifespans.
- Fuel Cells: Nanotechnology can enhance the performance of fuel cells by improving the efficiency of catalysts used in reactions.
- Nano-catalysts can provide more active sites for reactions to occur, leading to higher efficiency and lower costs for fuel cell systems, which are critical for clean energy applications.

2. Current Research and Future Possibilities

Nanotechnology is a rapidly evolving field, with ongoing research aimed at overcoming current limitations and unlocking new possibilities across various industries. The interdisciplinary nature of nanotechnology research brings together experts in physics, chemistry, biology, and engineering to push the boundaries of what is possible at the nanoscale.

A. Current Research Areas

- Cancer Treatment: One of the most promising areas of nanotechnology research is in the fight against cancer. Researchers are developing nanocarriers for targeted drug delivery, nano-biosensors for early detection, and nanoparticles that can enhance imaging techniques to better visualize tumors.
- Nanomedicine for Neurodegenerative Diseases: Nanotechnology is being explored as a potential treatment for neurodegenerative diseases such as Alzheimer's and Parkinson's. Nanoparticles can cross the blood-brain barrier and deliver drugs or genetic material directly to affected areas in the brain, offering new hope for treating these currently incurable diseases.
- Nano-photonics: This emerging field focuses on the interaction of light with nanoscale structures. Nano-photonics has applications in areas like telecommunications, quantum computing, and the development of ultrafast, highly efficient optical devices.

B. Future Possibilities

The future possibilities for nanotechnology are vast and transformative. As researchers continue to develop more sophisticated tools and techniques for manipulating materials at the atomic level, the potential applications of nanotechnology will expand in ways that are difficult to predict. Some of the most exciting future possibilities include:

- Artificial Organs: Nanotechnology could enable the creation of artificial organs that mimic the structure and function of natural organs, providing a solution to the shortage of organ donors and reducing the risk of rejection in transplant patients.
- Nanobots for Surgery: In the future, tiny robots operating at the nanoscale, known as nanobots, could perform highly precise surgeries inside the human body, repairing damaged tissues, clearing blockages, or even removing cancer cells without the need for invasive procedures.
- Space Exploration: Nanotechnology could play a key role in space exploration by enabling the development of lightweight, durable materials for spacecraft, as well as advanced life support systems for long-duration missions.
- Environmental Remediation: Nanotechnology could be used to clean up pollutants and toxins from the environment. Nanoparticles can be designed to bind to specific contaminants, making them easier to remove from soil or water.

Summary

Nanotechnology is a rapidly growing field that holds the potential to revolutionize industries ranging from medicine to energy. By working at the atomic and molecular levels, nanotechnology enables the creation of new materials, devices, and systems with unprecedented capabilities. As current research pushes the boundaries of what is possible, the future of nanotechnology promises exciting advancements that could solve some of the world's most pressing challenges. However, realizing the full potential of nanotechnology will require overcoming technical, ethical, and societal hurdles to ensure that its benefits are shared equitably and responsibly.

B. Economic Impacts of Nanotechnology

1. Potential for innovation in manufacturing and product development
2. Effects on existing industries and job markets

B. Economic Impacts of Nanotechnology

As nanotechnology advances and integrates into various sectors, its economic impacts are multifaceted and profound. The potential for innovation in manufacturing and product development is immense, promising to transform traditional practices and catalyze the emergence of new industries. However, these innovations also bring challenges to existing industries and job markets, necessitating a comprehensive examination of both the benefits and disruptions associated with nanotechnology's proliferation.

1. Potential for Innovation in Manufacturing and Product Development

Nanotechnology is reshaping manufacturing by enabling the creation of materials with enhanced properties, leading to significant improvements in product performance, efficiency, and sustainability. At the core of this transformation is the ability to manipulate matter at the nanoscale, allowing for the design of materials that can outperform their traditional counterparts.

A. Advanced Materials and Manufacturing Techniques

One of the most notable innovations driven by nanotechnology is the development of advanced materials. For example, nanocomposites, which incorporate nanoscale materials into traditional matrices, exhibit superior strength, lightness, and thermal stability. These materials are increasingly used in industries such as aerospace, automotive, and construction, where performance and weight are critical considerations.

Manufacturers are also adopting nanotechnology to improve production processes. Techniques like additive manufacturing (3D printing) benefit significantly from nanotechnology, allowing for the production of complex geometries and customized products with reduced waste and enhanced material efficiency. For instance, the use of nanoscale materials in 3D printing can lead to stronger, lighter components that can be tailored to specific applications.

B. Enhanced Product Performance

Nanotechnology enhances product performance across a wide range of applications. In electronics, nanoscale components enable faster, more efficient devices with lower power consumption. For example, transistors made from carbon nanotubes can outperform traditional silicon-based transistors, leading to faster computing speeds and smaller devices. As consumer electronics continue to shrink in size while increasing in functionality, nanotechnology plays a pivotal role in driving this evolution.

In the healthcare sector, nanotechnology facilitates the development of innovative drug delivery systems that improve therapeutic efficacy. Nanoparticles can be engineered to target specific cells or tissues, minimizing side effects and maximizing treatment effectiveness. Such advancements not only improve patient outcomes but also create new business opportunities within the pharmaceutical and biotechnology sectors.

C. Sustainability and Environmental Impact

Nanotechnology contributes to sustainability efforts by enabling more efficient resource utilization and reducing environmental footprints. For instance, nanotechnology can enhance energy efficiency in manufacturing processes, decreasing energy consumption and waste generation. Additionally, nanomaterials can be employed in environmental applications, such as water purification and pollution remediation, helping to address pressing ecological challenges.

The development of nanotechnology-driven renewable energy solutions, such as improved solar cells and energy storage systems, is another significant innovation. Nanostructured materials can enhance the efficiency and durability of solar panels, making renewable energy sources more competitive with fossil fuels. As society increasingly transitions towards sustainable practices, nanotechnology stands to play a central role in this transformation.

2. Effects on Existing Industries and Job Markets

While the innovations brought about by nanotechnology hold significant promise, they also pose challenges for existing industries and job markets. The integration of nanotechnology can lead to both disruptions and opportunities, necessitating a nuanced understanding of its economic implications.

A. Disruption of Traditional Industries

Many traditional industries face the prospect of disruption as nanotechnology changes the landscape of production and product development. For example, the materials industry must adapt to new nanocomposite materials that may render older materials obsolete. This shift could lead to reduced demand for traditional manufacturing processes, impacting industries such as steel, plastics, and textiles.

In the automotive sector, the integration of nanotechnology may alter supply chains as manufacturers seek to source advanced materials that enhance performance and reduce weight. Companies that do not adapt to these changes may struggle to remain competitive, leading to potential job losses and restructuring within the industry.

Similarly, the pharmaceutical industry faces significant transformation as nanotechnology enables new methods of drug delivery and personalized medicine. Companies that embrace these innovations may thrive, while those resistant to change could face challenges in maintaining market share.

B. Job Market Implications

The economic impacts of nanotechnology on job markets are complex and multifaceted. On one hand, the emergence of nanotechnology-driven industries presents opportunities for job creation in research, development, manufacturing, and regulatory compliance. Positions in nanotechnology research and engineering, as well as in sectors focusing on nanomedicine and advanced materials, are likely to expand as demand for expertise in this field grows.

However, the transition to a nanotechnology-driven economy may also lead to job displacement in traditional industries. Workers in sectors that are significantly disrupted may find themselves facing unemployment or the need to transition to new roles. For instance, those involved in manufacturing traditional materials may need to reskill to adapt to the production of advanced nanomaterials.

C. Workforce Development and Reskilling

To address the challenges posed by the integration of nanotechnology into various sectors, workforce development and reskilling will be crucial. Educational institutions, industry stakeholders, and policymakers must collaborate to develop training programs that equip workers with the necessary skills to thrive in an evolving job market.

Programs focusing on nanotechnology, materials science, and advanced manufacturing techniques will be essential in preparing the workforce for new opportunities. Additionally, fostering partnerships between educational institutions and industry can help ensure that curricula align with the skills needed in the job market.

Moreover, as industries evolve, there is an increasing demand for interdisciplinary expertise that spans various fields, including chemistry, physics, biology, and engineering. Encouraging a holistic approach to education can help bridge the skills gap and prepare workers for the complexities of a nanotechnology-driven economy.

Summary

The economic impacts of nanotechnology are profound, offering potential for innovation in manufacturing and product development while also posing challenges to existing industries and job markets. As nanotechnology continues to evolve, its ability to enhance materials, improve manufacturing processes, and contribute to sustainability efforts will play a crucial role in shaping the future economy. However, addressing the disruptions and transitions within the workforce will be essential to ensure that the benefits of nanotechnology are realized equitably and responsibly. By investing in education, reskilling initiatives, and fostering collaboration between industry and academia, society can navigate the challenges and embrace the opportunities presented by nanotechnology in the years to come.

C. Societal and Ethical Implications of Nanotechnology

1. Health and safety concerns
2. Environmental impact and regulatory challenges

C. Societal and Ethical Implications of Nanotechnology

As nanotechnology continues to develop and permeate various sectors, its societal and ethical implications have garnered significant attention. This section delves into two critical aspects of nanotechnology: health and safety concerns and environmental impacts, along with the associated regulatory challenges. Understanding these implications is vital for ensuring that the benefits of nanotechnology are harnessed responsibly and ethically.

1. Health and Safety Concerns

The introduction of nanotechnology in consumer products, industrial applications, and medical treatments raises numerous health and safety concerns that must be addressed. The unique properties of nanomaterials, derived from their nanoscale dimensions, can result in behaviors and interactions that differ significantly from their bulk counterparts. Consequently, these properties may pose risks to human health, necessitating a thorough assessment of potential hazards.

A. Potential Toxicity of Nanomaterials

One of the primary health concerns associated with nanotechnology is the potential toxicity of nanomaterials. Nanoparticles, due to their small size and high surface area-to-volume ratio, can exhibit increased reactivity and bioavailability.

Research indicates that certain nanomaterials, such as carbon nanotubes and metallic nanoparticles, may cause cytotoxic effects, inflammatory responses, or even genotoxicity when introduced into biological systems.

For example, studies have shown that inhaled nanoparticles can penetrate deep into lung tissues and enter the bloodstream, leading to systemic exposure. Additionally, some nanoparticles have been found to cross the blood-brain barrier, raising concerns about their effects on neurological health. These findings underscore the need for comprehensive toxicological assessments of nanomaterials to understand their potential health impacts and establish safe exposure limits.

B. Occupational Health Risks

The production and handling of nanomaterials can pose occupational health risks to workers in industries engaged in nanotechnology. Workers may be exposed to nanoparticles through inhalation, dermal contact, or ingestion during the manufacturing process. Given the uncertainty surrounding the long-term effects of nanomaterials, it is crucial to implement safety protocols and regulations to protect workers from potential hazards.

The Occupational Safety and Health Administration (OSHA) and other regulatory bodies must develop guidelines for the safe handling of nanomaterials in the workplace. This includes monitoring exposure levels, providing adequate personal protective equipment, and ensuring that workers are informed about potential risks associated with nanotechnology.

C. Consumer Safety and Product Regulation

As nanotechnology becomes increasingly integrated into consumer products, ensuring consumer safety is paramount. Products such as sunscreens, cosmetics, and food packaging often contain engineered nanomaterials, raising questions about their safety for public use. Regulatory agencies, including the Food and Drug Administration (FDA) and the Environmental Protection Agency (EPA), face challenges in evaluating the safety of nanotechnology applications due to the lack of comprehensive testing frameworks and guidelines specific to nanomaterials.

Regulatory frameworks must evolve to address the unique characteristics of nanomaterials, including their potential for bioaccumulation and persistence in the environment. Additionally, transparency in labeling nanotechnology-containing products can empower consumers to make informed choices about their safety.

2. Environmental Impact and Regulatory Challenges

Nanotechnology's potential benefits extend to environmental applications, such as pollution remediation and resource management. However, the introduction of nanomaterials into ecosystems raises important environmental concerns that must be addressed alongside their advantages. The potential for unintended consequences, combined with existing regulatory challenges, creates a complex landscape for managing nanotechnology's environmental impact.

A. Environmental Fate and Transport of Nanomaterials

Understanding the environmental fate and transport of nanomaterials is essential for assessing their potential impacts on ecosystems. Once released into the environment, nanoparticles can interact with soil, water, and air, leading to unknown consequences for biodiversity and ecological health.

Studies have shown that nanoparticles can alter the behavior of microorganisms, disrupt food webs, and accumulate in organisms through trophic transfer. The long-term effects of these interactions remain largely unexplored, necessitating extensive research into the environmental persistence and toxicity of nanomaterials.

B. Regulatory Frameworks and Challenges

The rapid pace of nanotechnology development poses significant challenges for regulatory frameworks designed to ensure environmental protection. Current regulations often lag behind technological advancements, creating gaps in oversight for nanomaterials. Many countries lack comprehensive regulations specifically addressing nanotechnology, which can lead to inconsistent safety standards and inadequate environmental protection.

Regulatory agencies face the daunting task of balancing the promotion of nanotechnology innovation with the necessity of protecting public health and the environment. This requires the development of adaptable regulatory frameworks that can accommodate the evolving nature of nanotechnology while ensuring rigorous safety assessments.

C. International Collaboration and Standards

Given the global nature of nanotechnology, international collaboration and standardization are essential for addressing its societal and environmental implications. Countries must work together to establish uniform safety standards, testing protocols, and regulatory guidelines for nanomaterials. This collaboration can foster knowledge sharing, enhance regulatory coherence, and promote responsible innovation.

Organizations such as the Organization for Economic Co-operation and Development (OECD) play a crucial role in facilitating international discussions on nanotechnology regulation. By fostering collaboration among governments, industry stakeholders, and researchers, it is possible to develop a comprehensive framework that addresses the ethical, health, and environmental concerns associated with nanotechnology.

Conclusion

The societal and ethical implications of nanotechnology are significant and multifaceted, encompassing health and safety concerns as well as environmental impacts and regulatory challenges. As nanotechnology continues to advance, it is imperative that stakeholders, including governments, industries, and researchers, collaborate to address these concerns effectively. By prioritizing safety assessments, establishing robust regulatory frameworks, and fostering international cooperation, society can harness the potential of nanotechnology while safeguarding public health and the environment. The responsible development and application of nanotechnology will be essential for realizing its benefits while minimizing risks, ultimately shaping a sustainable future for all.

V. Extended Reality (XR) and Virtual Reality (VR) Technologies

A. Overview of XR and VR technologies

1. Definitions and distinctions between VR, AR, and MR
2. Current applications in gaming, education, and training

A. Overview of XR and VR Technologies

Extended Reality (XR) is an umbrella term that encompasses a spectrum of immersive technologies, including Virtual Reality (VR), Augmented Reality (AR), and Mixed Reality (MR). Each of these technologies offers unique experiences that blend digital elements with the physical world, enabling users to interact with virtual environments and digital content in innovative ways. This section will delve into the definitions and distinctions between VR, AR, and MR, as well as their current applications in gaming, education, and training.

1. Definitions and Distinctions between VR, AR, and MR

Virtual Reality (VR) refers to a fully immersive digital environment that completely replaces the user's physical surroundings. Users *don* VR headsets, which immerse them in a computer-generated 3D world, allowing them to interact with the environment using hand controllers or body movements. The experience is designed to engage the user's senses, primarily vision and sound, creating a sense of presence in a virtual space. VR is commonly used in gaming, entertainment, therapy, and simulations.

Augmented Reality (AR) overlays digital information onto the real world, enhancing the user's perception of their environment. Unlike VR, which immerses users in a completely virtual setting, AR allows users to see and interact with both physical and digital elements simultaneously. This can be achieved through smartphone apps, smart glasses, or headsets. A popular example of AR is Pokémon GO, where players see virtual creatures superimposed on their real-world surroundings through their smartphone screens.

Mixed Reality (MR) combines elements of both VR and AR, allowing users to interact with digital content that is anchored to the physical world. MR systems use advanced sensors and displays to map the user's environment and integrate digital objects seamlessly within it. This means users can manipulate virtual objects as if they were part of the real world. Microsoft's HoloLens is a well-known example of MR technology, enabling users to interact with holographic projections that coexist with their physical environment.

Understanding these distinctions is crucial for recognizing the unique capabilities and applications of each technology, as well as their potential impacts on various sectors.

2. Current Applications in Gaming, Education, and Training

The applications of XR and VR technologies are vast, with significant advancements in sectors such as gaming, education, and training. Each area showcases the transformative potential of immersive technologies and how they can enhance user experiences and learning outcomes.

Gaming: The gaming industry has been at the forefront of VR and XR adoption, creating immersive experiences that engage players in unprecedented ways. VR gaming allows players to enter digital worlds, interact with characters and environments, and experience narratives from a first-person perspective. Titles like Beat Saber, Half-Life: Alyx, and The Walking Dead: Saints & Sinners demonstrate how VR can deliver thrilling, interactive experiences that transcend traditional gaming formats. Additionally, AR gaming, exemplified by Pokémon GO and Ingress, encourages players to explore their surroundings while engaging with virtual elements, fostering a unique blend of physical and digital interaction.

Education: XR technologies are revolutionizing education by providing immersive learning experiences that enhance engagement and understanding. In traditional learning environments, students often struggle to grasp complex concepts without tangible examples. XR technologies can bridge this gap by creating interactive simulations and visualizations that make abstract ideas more accessible. For instance, VR allows students to explore historical sites, conduct virtual science experiments, or experience biological processes up close, offering a hands-on approach to learning. AR can also enhance classroom learning by overlaying digital information onto physical textbooks or objects, allowing students to access additional resources and interactive content.

Training: XR technologies have emerged as powerful tools for training in various fields, including healthcare, aviation, military, and manufacturing. VR training simulations enable professionals to practice skills in controlled, risk-free environments, reducing the likelihood of errors in real-world scenarios. For example, medical students can conduct virtual surgeries, honing their skills without endangering patients. Similarly, pilots can utilize VR flight simulators to practice emergency procedures or flight maneuvers.

AR training applications can provide real-time instructions and guidance to workers in complex tasks, such as assembly line work or equipment maintenance, enhancing their efficiency and accuracy.

The integration of XR and VR technologies into gaming, education, and training not only enhances user experiences but also prepares individuals for the demands of an increasingly digital world. As these technologies continue to evolve, their applications will likely expand, reshaping various sectors and influencing how people learn, work, and interact with their environments.

Summary

Extended Reality (XR) and Virtual Reality (VR) technologies represent a significant evolution in how humans interact with digital content and the physical world. By understanding the distinctions between VR, AR, and MR, as well as their applications in gaming, education, and training, we can appreciate the transformative potential of these technologies. As XR and VR continue to advance, they will likely play an increasingly vital role in shaping experiences and opportunities across various sectors, paving the way for a more immersive and interconnected future. Embracing these technologies will be essential for harnessing their benefits while addressing the challenges they may pose in terms of accessibility, ethical considerations, and societal impacts.

B. Economic Impacts of Extended Reality (XR) and Virtual Reality (VR) Technologies

1. New opportunities in entertainment, education, and remote work
2. The rise of virtual economies and digital assets

B. Economic Impacts of Extended Reality (XR) and Virtual Reality (VR) Technologies

As Extended Reality (XR) and Virtual Reality (VR) technologies continue to evolve, they are reshaping various industries and creating significant economic impacts. From opening new avenues in entertainment and education to fostering remote work capabilities and generating virtual economies, these technologies are transforming the economic landscape. This section will explore new opportunities created by XR and VR in entertainment, education, and remote work, as well as the rise of virtual economies and digital assets.

1. New Opportunities in Entertainment, Education, and Remote Work

Entertainment:

The entertainment industry has been one of the most dynamic sectors to embrace XR and VR technologies. The immersive nature of these technologies allows for innovative storytelling and user engagement. VR experiences enable users to step into the narrative, offering a level of immersion that traditional media cannot match. For instance, VR gaming has seen substantial growth, with titles like "Beat Saber" and "Half-Life: Alyx" leading the charge. These games generate revenue not only through sales but also through subscription services, in-game purchases, and accessories such as VR headsets and controllers. Moreover, VR has found applications in theme parks, where visitors can engage in virtual rides and experiences, contributing to the growth of this niche market.

The film industry is also exploring VR, with studios producing immersive experiences that allow audiences to engage with storylines from multiple perspectives. Platforms like Oculus TV and Venues are beginning to host virtual film festivals, offering filmmakers new avenues to showcase their work and connect with audiences worldwide. Additionally, the integration of XR into live performances—such as concerts, theater productions, and sports events—has created novel experiences that enhance viewer engagement and attract new audiences.

Education:

XR technologies are revolutionizing education by providing immersive learning experiences that facilitate better understanding and retention of information. By simulating real-world scenarios, VR can transform how subjects like science, history, and art are taught. Educational institutions are increasingly adopting VR for subjects like medicine, where students can practice surgical procedures in a risk-free environment, allowing them to hone their skills without endangering patients. This approach is not only cost-effective but also enhances the learning experience, resulting in better-prepared professionals.

Additionally, AR applications are enriching classroom experiences by overlaying digital content onto physical materials, allowing for interactive lessons that cater to various learning styles. The demand for educational VR content is leading to the emergence of new businesses and startups focused on developing educational platforms and content, creating jobs and economic growth within the edtech sector.

Remote work has gained prominence in recent years, and XR technologies are playing a crucial role in enhancing virtual collaboration. Tools that incorporate VR and AR can facilitate immersive meetings and brainstorming sessions, allowing teams to collaborate as if they were in the same room. This shift toward remote work is contributing to reduced operational costs for businesses, as companies can maintain productivity without the need for physical office spaces. The demand for VR meeting platforms like Spatial and Gather is rapidly increasing, creating new business opportunities and revenue streams.

Remote Work:

The COVID-19 pandemic accelerated the shift to remote work, and XR technologies are increasingly being integrated into remote work environments to facilitate collaboration and productivity. Traditional video conferencing tools often fail to replicate the in-person experience, leading to feelings of isolation among remote workers. VR platforms provide immersive environments where team members can interact more naturally, leading to improved communication and collaboration.

For instance, platforms like VRChat and AltspaceVR allow users to create and customize avatars and interact in shared virtual spaces. These environments foster a sense of presence that traditional conferencing tools lack. Furthermore, businesses can benefit from reduced overhead costs associated with physical office spaces, enabling them to invest more in technology and employee development.

The growing demand for remote work solutions has led to increased investments in XR technologies, resulting in a burgeoning market for software and hardware development. As companies seek to enhance productivity and employee satisfaction, the economic potential of XR and VR technologies in remote work environments will likely continue to expand.

2. The Rise of Virtual Economies and Digital Assets

The emergence of XR and VR technologies has given rise to new economic models, particularly in the realm of virtual economies and digital assets. These economies are characterized by the creation and exchange of digital goods, services, and experiences within virtual environments, often leveraging blockchain technology and cryptocurrencies.

Virtual Economies:

As more individuals engage with virtual worlds, the demand for digital goods and services is skyrocketing. Virtual economies allow users to buy, sell, and trade digital assets, such as virtual real estate, clothing for avatars, and in-game items. Platforms like *Decentraland* and Second Life exemplify this trend, where users can create, buy, and sell virtual properties, art, and experiences. These economies are generating real-world income for individuals and businesses, contributing to the overall economic landscape.

Moreover, the rise of *non-fungible tokens* (NFTs) has transformed the way digital assets are valued and exchanged. NFTs are unique digital tokens that represent ownership of a specific item or piece of content, whether it's artwork, music, or virtual collectibles. The NFT market has exploded in popularity, with artists and creators leveraging these technologies to monetize their work. This trend not only benefits creators but also attracts investors looking to capitalize on the growing interest in digital assets.

Digital Assets:

Digital assets, including cryptocurrencies, are becoming increasingly integrated into virtual economies. Cryptocurrencies provide a decentralized medium of exchange that enables transactions within virtual environments without the need for traditional financial systems. For instance, in-game currencies are often used in gaming platforms to facilitate transactions for digital goods, while cryptocurrencies can be utilized to purchase virtual real estate or artwork in platforms like Decentraland.

The growth of digital assets is driving the development of blockchain technology, which enhances the security and transparency of transactions. This has significant implications for various sectors, as businesses increasingly explore how blockchain can streamline processes and reduce costs. The rise of decentralized finance (DeFi) is also reshaping financial systems, offering alternative methods for lending, borrowing, and trading assets.

The impact of XR and VR technologies on virtual economies and digital assets will likely continue to grow as more users engage with these platforms. As economic activities transition into virtual spaces, businesses will need to adapt to new models and explore the opportunities presented by digital assets and currencies.

Summary

The economic impacts of Extended Reality (XR) and Virtual Reality (VR) technologies are far-reaching, creating new opportunities in entertainment, education, and remote work while fostering the emergence of virtual economies and digital assets. These technologies are not only transforming how industries operate but are also reshaping consumer behavior and expectations. As XR and VR continue to advance, their influence on the global economy will likely expand, prompting businesses and individuals to adapt to the evolving landscape. Embracing these technologies will be essential for harnessing their potential, driving innovation, and fostering economic growth in the digital age.

C. Societal Considerations of Extended Reality (XR) and Virtual Reality (VR) Technologies

1. Effects on social interactions and mental health
2. Ethical considerations regarding immersive experiences

Societal Considerations

As Extended Reality (XR) and Virtual Reality (VR) technologies continue to integrate into our daily lives, they bring with them a range of societal considerations. These technologies not only reshape the way we interact with one another but also have profound implications for mental health and well-being. Furthermore, as immersive experiences become more prevalent, ethical concerns arise regarding their potential effects on individuals and society at large. This section will delve into the effects of XR and VR on social interactions and mental health, as well as the ethical considerations that accompany immersive experiences.

1. Effects on Social Interactions and Mental Health

Changes in Social Dynamics

The integration of XR and VR technologies into our social lives has led to significant changes in how we interact with one another. Virtual environments provide opportunities for socialization that transcend geographical boundaries, allowing people to connect and engage in ways that were previously unimaginable. For instance, platforms like *VRChat* and *AltspaceVR* enable users to create avatars and interact in virtual spaces, fostering a sense of community and belonging among users who may feel isolated in the real world.

While these technologies can enhance social connections, they also raise concerns about the quality of interactions. Virtual interactions may lack the emotional nuances of face-to-face communication, which can lead to misunderstandings and feelings of alienation. Moreover, the proliferation of virtual identities can complicate social dynamics, as users may present curated versions of themselves, leading to dissonance between their online and offline personas. This disconnection from reality can have adverse effects on interpersonal relationships, leading to a decline in the quality of real-world social interactions.

Mental Health Implications

The impact of XR and VR on mental health is a complex and multifaceted issue. On one hand, these technologies can serve as powerful tools for therapeutic interventions. For example, VR has been employed in exposure therapy for individuals suffering from anxiety disorders, phobias, and post-traumatic stress disorder (PTSD). By immersing patients in controlled virtual environments, therapists can help them confront their fears in a safe space, facilitating healing and recovery.

Additionally, VR can provide an escape from the stresses of everyday life, offering users a chance to immerse themselves in alternate realities and experiences. This can be particularly beneficial for individuals dealing with mental health challenges, as it allows for temporary respite and relaxation. However, the effectiveness of these experiences hinges on moderation and balance. Excessive use of XR and VR technologies can lead to social withdrawal, increased feelings of loneliness, and a diminished capacity for real-world interactions.

Research has indicated that prolonged engagement with virtual environments can contribute to a phenomenon known as "presence," where users feel a strong emotional connection to their virtual experiences. While this can enhance engagement, it may also lead to adverse mental health outcomes if users become overly attached to their virtual lives at the expense of their real-world relationships and responsibilities. The immersive nature of these technologies can blur the lines between reality and virtuality, potentially leading to escapism and detachment from real-life issues.

2. Ethical Considerations Regarding Immersive Experiences

The Nature of Reality and Identity

As XR and VR technologies continue to develop, they prompt critical ethical questions about the nature of reality and identity. Immersive experiences can challenge our understanding of what it means to be human and how we define ourselves. The ability to create and inhabit virtual identities raises concerns about authenticity and self-perception. Users may struggle to reconcile their virtual experiences with their real-world identities, leading to questions about the impact of these technologies on self-esteem and body image.

Moreover, the potential for identity manipulation in virtual environments introduces ethical dilemmas surrounding consent and representation. For instance, users may assume avatars that do not accurately reflect their physical selves, raising concerns about cultural appropriation and misrepresentation. These issues are particularly pertinent in social interactions, where users may mislead others about their identities, leading to trust issues and ethical quandaries in online communities.

Privacy and Data Security

The immersive nature of XR and VR technologies necessitates the collection and analysis of vast amounts of user data, including biometric information and behavioral patterns. This raises significant ethical concerns regarding privacy and data security. As users engage with virtual environments, their interactions, preferences, and emotional responses may be monitored and analyzed by companies for various purposes, including targeted advertising and user profiling.

The potential for misuse of personal data is a pressing issue, as it can lead to exploitation, manipulation, and the erosion of individual privacy. Users may not fully understand the extent of data collection occurring in virtual environments or the potential consequences of sharing their information. Ethical considerations must be taken into account to ensure that users are informed about how their data is being used and that their privacy is protected.

Regulation and Responsibility

As XR and VR technologies continue to gain traction, there is a pressing need for regulatory frameworks to address the ethical implications of immersive experiences. Policymakers, technologists, and ethicists must work together to establish guidelines that prioritize user safety, privacy, and well-being. This includes developing industry standards for data protection, informed consent, and ethical design principles that prioritize user experience.

Moreover, companies developing XR and VR technologies have a responsibility to consider the societal impact of their products. Ethical considerations should be embedded in the design process to ensure that technologies are developed with the well-being of users in mind. This includes addressing potential risks, fostering inclusive environments, and promoting healthy usage patterns.

Conclusion

The societal considerations surrounding Extended Reality (XR) and Virtual Reality (VR) technologies are complex and multifaceted. While these technologies offer unprecedented opportunities for social interaction and mental health interventions, they also raise critical questions about the quality of those interactions and the potential impact on mental well-being. Ethical considerations regarding identity, privacy, and data security must be carefully navigated to ensure that users can engage with these technologies in a safe and responsible manner. As XR and VR continue to evolve, it will be essential to foster a dialogue among stakeholders to address these concerns and promote the development of immersive experiences that enhance rather than hinder societal well-being.

VI. Cryptocurrencies and Future Currencies

A. Definition and evolution of cryptocurrencies

1. Overview of major cryptocurrencies (Bitcoin, Ethereum, etc.)
2. The rise of decentralized finance (DeFi) and non-fungible tokens (NFTs)

A. Definition and Evolution of Cryptocurrencies

1. Overview of Major Cryptocurrencies

Cryptocurrencies are digital or virtual currencies that use cryptography for security, making them resistant to counterfeiting and fraud. The decentralized nature of most cryptocurrencies, which are based on blockchain technology, distinguishes them from traditional currencies issued by governments and regulated by central banks. Since the inception of Bitcoin in 2009, cryptocurrencies have evolved significantly, giving rise to various digital currencies with distinct characteristics, purposes, and applications.

Bitcoin (BTC)

Bitcoin, created by an anonymous individual or group known as Satoshi Nakamoto, is widely regarded as the first and most well-known cryptocurrency. It was initially designed as a peer-to-peer digital cash system that allows users to conduct transactions without the need for intermediaries, such as banks. Bitcoin operates on a decentralized network of computers (nodes) that validate and record transactions on a public ledger called the blockchain. This system ensures transparency and security, as each transaction is verified by network participants through a process called mining, which involves solving complex mathematical puzzles to add new blocks to the chain.

Bitcoin's primary appeal lies in its deflationary design, with a maximum supply cap of 21 million coins. This limited supply, combined with its decentralized nature, has led many to view Bitcoin as "digital gold" and a potential hedge against inflation. Over the years, Bitcoin has gained traction not only as a speculative asset but also as a means of transferring value globally, especially in regions with unstable financial systems or limited access to traditional banking services.

Ethereum (ETH)

While Bitcoin is primarily focused on digital currency, Ethereum takes blockchain technology further by enabling the creation of decentralized applications (dApps) and smart contracts. Launched in 2015 by Vitalik Buterin and his team, Ethereum is a decentralized platform that allows developers to build and deploy smart contracts—self-executing contracts with the terms directly written into code. These contracts automatically execute transactions when predefined conditions are met, removing the need for intermediaries like lawyers or notaries.

Ethereum's native cryptocurrency, Ether (ETH), is used to fuel the network and compensate miners for validating transactions and executing smart contracts. Ethereum's flexibility and programmability have made it the foundation for a wide range of decentralized applications, including decentralized finance (DeFi) platforms, gaming ecosystems, and non-fungible tokens (NFTs). Ethereum has played a pivotal role in shaping the blockchain landscape, with many innovative projects leveraging its infrastructure to create new use cases for blockchain technology.

Other Cryptocurrencies

In addition to Bitcoin and Ethereum, there are thousands of other cryptocurrencies, often referred to as altcoins, each with its own unique features and applications. Some notable examples include:

- Ripple (XRP): A digital payment protocol designed to facilitate fast, low-cost international money transfers.
- Litecoin (LTC): A peer-to-peer cryptocurrency that offers faster transaction times and lower fees than Bitcoin.
- Cardano (ADA): A blockchain platform focused on scalability, sustainability, and interoperability, with a strong emphasis on academic research and peer-reviewed development.
- Polkadot (DOT): A multi-chain platform that enables different blockchains to interoperate and share information securely.

Each of these cryptocurrencies has carved out a niche in the digital currency ecosystem, contributing to the ongoing evolution of the cryptocurrency market and expanding the possibilities for decentralized finance and digital ownership.

2. The Rise of Decentralized Finance (DeFi) and Non-Fungible Tokens (NFTs)

Decentralized Finance (DeFi)

Decentralized finance, or DeFi, refers to a broad range of financial services and products that are built on blockchain technology and operate without the need for traditional financial intermediaries, such as banks or brokers. DeFi aims to democratize access to financial services by creating decentralized, permissionless platforms that allow users to lend, borrow, trade, and invest in assets directly with one another. The underlying infrastructure of DeFi is typically built on the Ethereum blockchain, although other blockchain networks are starting to gain traction in the space.

One of the core components of DeFi is decentralized exchanges (DEXs), which allow users to trade cryptocurrencies directly with one another without relying on centralized exchanges. Other DeFi services include lending protocols, such as Aave and Compound, which enable users to earn interest on their assets or borrow against them using cryptocurrency as collateral. Stablecoins, which are cryptocurrencies pegged to a stable asset like the US dollar, also play a crucial role in DeFi by providing a reliable medium of exchange and store of value within the ecosystem.

DeFi has experienced explosive growth in recent years, attracting billions of dollars in total value locked (TVL) in smart contracts. The transparency and programmability of blockchain technology allow for innovative financial products, such as yield farming (earning returns by providing liquidity to DeFi platforms) and flash loans (unsecured loans that must be repaid within a single transaction). However, DeFi also presents risks, including smart contract vulnerabilities, market volatility, and the potential for regulatory scrutiny.

Non-Fungible Tokens (NFTs)

Non-fungible tokens (NFTs) are unique digital assets that represent ownership of a specific item, piece of content, or asset on the blockchain. Unlike cryptocurrencies such as Bitcoin or Ether, which are fungible and interchangeable, NFTs are one-of-a-kind and cannot be replicated. This uniqueness has made NFTs particularly popular in industries such as digital art, music, gaming, and collectibles.

NFTs are typically created and traded on blockchain platforms like Ethereum, where smart contracts ensure that ownership and provenance are verifiable and transparent. The use of NFTs allows artists, musicians, and creators to tokenize their work, providing new revenue streams and enabling direct engagement with their audience.

For example, a digital artist can mint an NFT representing a piece of artwork and sell it to a buyer, who then holds the unique token proving ownership of the original digital file.

The NFT market has witnessed significant growth, with high-profile sales reaching millions of dollars. However, the space is still evolving, and there are ongoing debates about the environmental impact of NFT minting (due to the energy-intensive nature of some blockchains) and concerns about the speculative nature of the market. Despite these challenges, NFTs have the potential to revolutionize the way we think about ownership, intellectual property, and the digital economy.

Summary

Cryptocurrencies and the broader blockchain ecosystem, including DeFi and NFTs, represent a paradigm shift in the way we approach finance, ownership, and value exchange. Major cryptocurrencies like Bitcoin and Ethereum have laid the foundation for decentralized financial systems and programmable digital assets, while emerging technologies like DeFi and NFTs continue to push the boundaries of what is possible. As these innovations evolve, they will play a critical role in shaping the future of the global economy, creating new opportunities for investment, commerce, and the reimagining of traditional financial systems. Understanding the definition and evolution of these technologies is essential to grasping their potential impact on both the current and future economy.

B. Economic implications of Cryptocurrencies

1. Impact on traditional banking and financial systems
2. Potential for increased economic inclusivity and access to capital

The rise of cryptocurrencies and decentralized financial technologies has profound economic implications that could reshape traditional banking, financial systems, and access to capital. While still in its early stages, the impact of cryptocurrencies extends beyond merely offering an alternative form of money; it challenges the very structure of existing financial institutions and has the potential to bring financial inclusivity to underserved populations.

1. Impact on Traditional Banking and Financial Systems

The introduction of cryptocurrencies, particularly Bitcoin and Ethereum, has sparked debates on the future role of traditional banking institutions. Cryptocurrencies operate on decentralized networks, meaning they do not rely on a central authority, such as a bank or government, to validate transactions. This decentralization represents a significant departure from conventional financial systems, which depend on intermediaries to manage the flow of money, regulate markets, and enforce monetary policy. The result is a potential disruption to the banking sector, especially as cryptocurrencies become more integrated into everyday transactions and global finance.

Disintermediation of Financial Services

One of the most significant ways cryptocurrencies impact traditional banking is through the concept of disintermediation. Disintermediation refers to the removal of intermediaries from a process—in this case, the removal of banks, brokers, and financial institutions from monetary transactions. Blockchain technology, which underpins most cryptocurrencies, allows peer-to-peer transfers of value without the need for a central party to verify or approve the transaction.

In the traditional banking system, financial institutions act as intermediaries for a range of services, such as processing payments, providing loans, and managing investments. Cryptocurrencies offer a more direct approach, where individuals can send or receive payments, lend money, or engage in investment opportunities directly through decentralized platforms. This disintermediation threatens the core business models of banks, as they may lose their central role in facilitating transactions. For example, decentralized finance (DeFi) protocols, built on blockchains like Ethereum, provide lending, borrowing, and trading services without requiring a central bank, making financial services more accessible to users worldwide.

Reduced Transaction Costs and Increased Efficiency

One of the touted advantages of cryptocurrencies is their potential to lower transaction costs, particularly for cross-border payments. Traditional international transfers involve multiple intermediaries, such as correspondent banks and payment processors, each adding fees and delays to the transaction. Cryptocurrencies, on the other hand, allow for near-instantaneous transactions across borders at a fraction of the cost, as they bypass the complex web of intermediaries.

For example, remittance services—where workers send money to their home countries—are particularly expensive through traditional banking systems. Companies like Western Union and MoneyGram charge significant fees for these services, which can be a heavy financial burden on those transferring small amounts of money. Cryptocurrencies can streamline this process, offering faster and cheaper solutions. The World Bank estimates that the average cost of sending remittances is around 7%, but blockchain-based solutions could reduce this significantly, fostering economic opportunities in developing nations that rely heavily on remittance income.

Monetary Policy and Sovereignty Concerns

Cryptocurrencies, particularly those with fixed supplies like Bitcoin, pose challenges to government control over monetary policy. Central banks control national currencies by influencing interest rates, printing money, and regulating money supply to stabilize economies and promote growth. However, decentralized cryptocurrencies operate independently of central bank control, reducing the ability of governments to influence the economy through traditional monetary tools.

A widely adopted cryptocurrency could limit central banks' ability to manage inflation, implement monetary stimulus, or devalue a currency to boost exports. Some governments have already expressed concerns about cryptocurrencies undermining national sovereignty over money. Countries like China have responded by banning Bitcoin mining and transactions, while simultaneously developing their own digital currencies, known as Central Bank Digital Currencies (CBDCs). These government-backed digital currencies aim to incorporate the advantages of cryptocurrencies, such as lower transaction costs and greater financial inclusion, while maintaining state control over monetary policy.

Increased Competition for Traditional Banks

Cryptocurrencies and the blockchain ecosystem also introduce new competition for *traditional banks* in the form of financial technology (FinTech) startups. Blockchain-based startups are developing innovative solutions that target various banking services, such as payments, lending, and investment management. These FinTech companies can offer lower fees, faster processing times, and more transparent services than traditional financial institutions, drawing customers away from banks.

For instance, decentralized finance platforms like *Aave* and Compound provide decentralized lending and borrowing services without the need for banks. Users can deposit their cryptocurrencies as collateral and borrow against them or lend their assets to earn interest through automated smart contracts. These DeFi platforms pose a direct threat to the traditional lending and savings models offered by banks. As DeFi continues to evolve, it could create a parallel financial system that operates independently of traditional banks.

2. Potential for Increased Economic Inclusivity and Access to Capital

While cryptocurrencies may disrupt traditional financial institutions, they also offer the potential to increase financial inclusion and provide access to capital for underserved populations. The decentralized nature of cryptocurrencies allows individuals in regions with limited banking infrastructure to participate in the global economy, fostering greater economic participation and empowerment.

Financial Inclusion in Developing Markets

One of the most transformative aspects of cryptocurrencies is their ability to provide financial services to the unbanked and underbanked populations. According to the World Bank, approximately 1.7 billion adults globally are unbanked, meaning they do not have access to traditional financial services like bank accounts, loans, or credit. In many cases, individuals in developing regions face barriers to accessing financial institutions due to geographical isolation, lack of infrastructure, or exclusion from the formal economy.

Cryptocurrencies and blockchain technology can help bridge this gap by offering decentralized, digital solutions that do not require individuals to rely on banks. All that is needed to access the cryptocurrency ecosystem is a smartphone and an internet connection, allowing users to send and receive payments, save money, and engage in commerce without needing a bank account. Additionally, decentralized finance platforms can offer microloans to individuals and small businesses in developing regions, providing access to capital that would otherwise be unavailable.

In countries experiencing economic instability, such as hyperinflation or political turmoil, cryptocurrencies also offer an alternative store of value. In places like Venezuela and Zimbabwe, where local currencies have experienced extreme devaluation, individuals have turned to Bitcoin and other cryptocurrencies as a means of preserving their wealth and accessing international markets. This ability to bypass unstable national currencies offers a lifeline to those in economically distressed regions, providing greater financial resilience and security.

Democratizing Investment Opportunities

Cryptocurrencies and decentralized finance platforms also democratize access to investment opportunities. Traditional financial systems often limit access to capital markets to wealthy individuals or those with established relationships with financial institutions. Cryptocurrencies, on the other hand, allow anyone with an internet connection to invest in a wide range of assets, from cryptocurrencies themselves to tokenized real estate, commodities, and stocks.

Through blockchain technology, fractional ownership of assets becomes possible, enabling individuals to invest in portions of expensive assets, such as real estate or rare art, without needing large sums of capital. This fractionalization reduces barriers to entry and opens up new opportunities for wealth creation, particularly for those who have historically been excluded from investment markets.

Challenges to Inclusivity

While cryptocurrencies have the potential to increase financial inclusion, challenges remain. Many blockchain platforms require a certain level of technological literacy, and the volatility of cryptocurrencies can deter individuals from adopting them as a stable store of value. Additionally, regulatory uncertainty surrounding cryptocurrencies in many countries creates risks for users and could lead to restrictions that limit access to these financial innovations. Ensuring that cryptocurrencies and decentralized finance platforms are user-friendly, secure, and widely accessible will be key to realizing their potential for economic inclusivity.

Summary

Cryptocurrencies are poised to have a profound impact on traditional banking and financial systems, challenging the role of intermediaries, reducing transaction costs, and reshaping monetary policy. At the same time, they offer opportunities for increased financial inclusion and access to capital, particularly in regions where traditional financial services are limited. As the world continues to embrace blockchain technology and decentralized finance, the economic implications of cryptocurrencies will become increasingly apparent, creating both challenges and opportunities for individuals, businesses, and governments alike. Understanding these dynamics will be crucial for navigating the evolving landscape of global finance in the digital age.

C. Challenges and considerations

1. Regulatory concerns and market volatility
2. Security risks and potential for misuse

C. Challenges and Considerations

Cryptocurrencies, while offering substantial potential for economic innovation and inclusion, also present several significant challenges that must be addressed for their widespread adoption. These challenges include regulatory concerns, market volatility, security risks, and the potential for misuse. Understanding these issues is crucial for ensuring that cryptocurrencies can be integrated into the global economy in a safe and sustainable manner. This section explores these challenges in detail.

1. Regulatory Concerns and Market Volatility

Regulatory Ambiguity and Legal Uncertainty

One of the most pressing challenges facing the cryptocurrency sector is the lack of a clear, consistent regulatory framework across different countries. Cryptocurrencies operate across borders and can be traded globally, making it difficult for any single government to enforce regulations effectively. While some nations, such as Japan and Switzerland, have adopted relatively clear and favorable regulatory frameworks, others, including China and India, have enacted outright bans or imposed severe restrictions on cryptocurrency activities.

In many countries, regulatory ambiguity creates uncertainty for businesses and investors. For instance, the classification of cryptocurrencies can vary: some countries treat them as commodities, others as currencies or securities. This inconsistent approach complicates tax reporting, investment decisions, and legal compliance for individuals and businesses involved in cryptocurrency activities.

In the United States, regulatory bodies such as the Securities and Exchange Commission (SEC) and the Commodity Futures Trading Commission (CFTC) have been struggling to develop a cohesive regulatory stance. The SEC, for instance, has taken action against some initial coin offerings (ICOs), considering them unregistered securities, while allowing other cryptocurrencies like Bitcoin and Ethereum to operate freely.

This piecemeal approach creates uncertainty for market participants, as they do not have clear guidelines about what activities are permissible or which tokens might be classified as securities in the future.

Furthermore, as the global adoption of decentralized finance (DeFi) and non-fungible tokens (NFTs) grows, the regulatory landscape will need to evolve to address the unique characteristics of these technologies. Many of these decentralized platforms operate without traditional intermediaries, raising questions about accountability and compliance with anti-money laundering (AML) and know-your-customer (KYC) regulations. Without clear guidance, the cryptocurrency market risks either over-regulation, which could stifle innovation, or under-regulation, which could lead to fraud, market manipulation, and financial instability.

Market Volatility and Financial Stability

Cryptocurrency markets are notorious for their extreme volatility, which presents a major barrier to their acceptance as a stable medium of exchange or store of value. While traditional currencies are typically subject to fluctuations of a few percentage points over long periods, cryptocurrencies like Bitcoin and Ethereum can experience price swings of 10% or more in a single day. This volatility makes it difficult for consumers and businesses to use cryptocurrencies for everyday transactions and hampers their ability to function as a stable alternative to fiat currencies.

The volatility of cryptocurrency markets is driven by a variety of factors, including speculative trading, regulatory news, technological developments, and market sentiment. For example, when major countries announce new regulatory restrictions on cryptocurrencies, it can trigger sharp price drops, as seen when China banned cryptocurrency transactions in 2021, causing

Bitcoin's value to plummet by nearly 30% within days. Conversely, positive developments, such as large companies announcing their acceptance of cryptocurrency payments, can cause prices to soar.

This volatility creates risks not only for individual investors but also for broader financial markets. If cryptocurrency markets continue to grow, there is a concern that they could contribute to financial instability, especially if traditional financial institutions become more exposed to cryptocurrency assets. Additionally, the rise of stablecoins—cryptocurrencies pegged to the value of traditional currencies or assets—has created new regulatory challenges, as some stablecoins have experienced significant price fluctuations or liquidity crises, raising concerns about their reliability as a stable asset class.

Governments and central banks are also concerned about the potential for cryptocurrencies to disrupt their ability to manage monetary policy and ensure financial stability. As more individuals and businesses move away from traditional currencies, central banks could lose some of their influence over the economy, particularly in controlling inflation, managing interest rates, and stabilizing national currencies.

To mitigate these risks, many countries are exploring the development of central bank digital currencies (CBDCs) as a way to offer the benefits of digital currencies while maintaining regulatory oversight and control over monetary policy.

2. Security Risks and Potential for Misuse

Hacking and Theft

One of the most significant security risks facing the cryptocurrency ecosystem is the vulnerability of digital assets to hacking and theft. Unlike traditional banking systems, where deposits are insured and transactions can be reversed in the event of fraud, cryptocurrency transactions are generally irreversible, and once funds are transferred, they cannot be recovered. This makes cryptocurrencies an attractive target for cybercriminals.

Several high-profile cryptocurrency exchanges and platforms have been hacked over the years, resulting in the theft of millions of dollars' worth of digital assets. For example, the Mt. Gox exchange, one of the largest Bitcoin exchanges in the world at the time, was hacked in 2014, leading to the loss of approximately 850,000 Bitcoins, valued at over $450 million at the time. More recently, in 2021, the Poly Network, a decentralized finance platform, was hacked, resulting in the theft of over $600 million worth of cryptocurrencies, although the hacker later returned the majority of the funds.

These incidents highlight the need for stronger security measures and better regulation of cryptocurrency platforms. Many exchanges and wallet providers have taken steps to improve their security, such as implementing multi-factor authentication, cold storage for assets, and encryption technologies. However, the decentralized nature of cryptocurrencies means that there is no central authority responsible for ensuring security, making it difficult to prevent and respond to theft or fraud.

The Dark Web and Illicit Activities

Another concern is the use of cryptocurrencies for illegal activities, particularly on the dark web, where anonymity and decentralization make it difficult for authorities to track and trace transactions. Cryptocurrencies such as Bitcoin and Monero have been used to facilitate illegal activities, including drug trafficking, money laundering, and ransomware attacks. For instance, the notorious Silk Road marketplace, which was shut down by the FBI in 2013, allowed users to purchase illicit goods using Bitcoin, taking advantage of the anonymity offered by the cryptocurrency.

Ransomware attacks, in which cybercriminals demand payment in cryptocurrencies in exchange for releasing hacked data, have also become increasingly common. In 2021, the Colonial Pipeline ransomware attack caused fuel shortages across the eastern United States, with the attackers demanding a ransom of approximately $4.4 million in Bitcoin. While law enforcement was able to recover a portion of the ransom, the incident underscored the role of cryptocurrencies in enabling cybercrime.

The pseudonymous nature of many cryptocurrencies makes it challenging for law enforcement agencies to trace and prosecute individuals involved in illegal activities. While blockchain technology provides a public ledger of all transactions, many users take steps to obfuscate their identities through the use of mixing services, privacy coins, or multiple wallets. This creates significant challenges for governments attempting to regulate the use of cryptocurrencies and prevent their misuse.

Regulatory and Technological Solutions to Security Risks

To address these security concerns, governments and regulatory bodies are increasingly turning to anti-money laundering (AML) and know-your-customer (KYC) regulations. These regulations require cryptocurrency exchanges and platforms to verify the identities of their users and report suspicious transactions to authorities. While these measures help to reduce the risk of cryptocurrencies being used for illegal activities, they are not foolproof, and many decentralized platforms, such as DeFi protocols, operate without traditional intermediaries, making it difficult to enforce compliance.

In addition to regulatory efforts, there are ongoing technological innovations aimed at improving the security of cryptocurrency systems. For instance, the development of quantum-resistant cryptographic algorithms is a key area of research, as the advent of quantum computing could potentially break the encryption methods that underpin most cryptocurrencies today.

Furthermore, the use of decentralized autonomous organizations (DAOs) and smart contracts could provide greater transparency and accountability in the cryptocurrency ecosystem, reducing the risk of fraud or misuse.

Conclusion

The rise of cryptocurrencies presents both opportunities and challenges for the global economy. While offering the potential for greater financial inclusion, reduced transaction costs, and new investment opportunities, cryptocurrencies also pose significant regulatory, security, and ethical challenges. Addressing these issues will be critical for ensuring that cryptocurrencies can be integrated into the global financial system in a way that promotes economic growth while minimizing the risks of misuse and financial instability. By developing clear regulatory frameworks, improving security measures, and fostering innovation, governments and the private sector can work together to create a sustainable and secure future for digital currencies.

Nuclear fusion is and how it can benefit society as a whole.

Understanding Clean Energy from Nuclear Fusion and Its Societal Benefits

1. **What Is Nuclear Fusion?**

Nuclear fusion is the process by which two atomic nuclei merge to form a heavier nucleus, releasing vast amounts of energy in the process. This reaction powers the sun and other stars, where hydrogen atoms fuse into helium under immense pressure and temperature. Unlike nuclear fission, which splits atoms and is used in conventional nuclear power plants, fusion produces no long-lived radioactive waste and has virtually unlimited fuel sources.

2. **The Science Behind Nuclear Fusion**

At extremely high temperatures (over 100 million degrees Celsius), hydrogen isotopes such as deuterium and tritium overcome electrostatic repulsion and collide with enough force to fuse into helium. This process releases energy in the form of kinetic energy of the reaction products, which can be harnessed to generate electricity. The key challenge is achieving the necessary conditions for sustained fusion reactions on Earth.

3. **Fuel Sources: Abundant and Accessible**

Fusion primarily uses deuterium, which can be extracted from seawater, and tritium, which can be bred from lithium. The oceans contain enough deuterium to power humanity for millions of years, making fusion a sustainable energy source. Unlike fossil fuels or uranium for fission reactors, fusion fuel is virtually inexhaustible.

4. **Energy Output: Greater Than Fossil Fuels**

A single gram of fusion fuel can generate as much energy as several tons of coal, oil, or natural gas. This efficiency means that fusion has the potential to replace all traditional energy sources while significantly reducing environmental impact.

5. **No Greenhouse Gas Emissions**

Unlike fossil fuels, nuclear fusion does not produce carbon dioxide (CO_2) or other greenhouse gases. This means fusion energy can play a crucial role in combating climate change by providing a clean, sustainable alternative to carbon-emitting power sources.

6. **Minimal Radioactive Waste**

Unlike nuclear fission, which generates long-lived radioactive waste, fusion produces very little radioactive material, and what it does produce has a much shorter half-life. This greatly reduces concerns about nuclear waste storage and environmental contamination.

7. **Intrinsic Safety: No Meltdown Risk**

One of the biggest advantages of fusion over fission is its inherent safety. Fusion reactions require extreme conditions to sustain themselves. If these conditions are disrupted, the reaction stops immediately—unlike fission reactors, which can overheat and lead to catastrophic meltdowns (e.g., Chernobyl, Fukushima).

8. **Energy Independence for Nations**

Countries that currently depend on imported fossil fuels could achieve energy independence through fusion. This would reduce geopolitical tensions over energy resources and stabilize global energy markets.

9. **Job Creation and Economic Growth**

The development and commercialization of fusion energy will create millions of jobs in engineering, construction, and research. It will also stimulate industries related to high-temperature materials, superconductors, and advanced energy storage solutions.

10. **Revolutionizing Space Exploration**

Fusion power could provide high-energy propulsion systems for interplanetary travel, enabling faster, more efficient space missions. Unlike chemical or fission-based propulsion, fusion offers high power-to-weight ratios, making long-term space colonization feasible.

11. **Applications Beyond Electricity Generation**

Beyond power plants, fusion energy can be used in hydrogen production, desalination, and industrial heating processes. This could lead to clean water supplies in arid regions and reduce reliance on fossil fuels in manufacturing.

12. **The Challenge of Achieving Break-even Energy**

One of the key hurdles in fusion research is achieving break-even energy, where the energy output exceeds the energy required to sustain the reaction. Projects like ITER (International Thermonuclear Experimental Reactor) and private-sector initiatives are working to overcome this challenge.

13. **Advances in Tokamaks and Stellarators**

The most promising fusion reactor designs include tokamaks (doughnut-shaped magnetic confinement reactors) and stellarators (twisting magnetic field designs). Improvements in superconducting magnets and plasma stability have brought commercial fusion closer to reality.

14. **The Rise of Laser and Inertial Confinement Fusion**

Another approach, inertial confinement fusion, uses high-powered lasers to compress fuel pellets to fusion conditions. The National Ignition Facility (NIF) in the U.S. recently demonstrated a small-scale net energy gain, marking a significant milestone.

15. **Fusion and Grid Integration**

For fusion to be viable, it must integrate with existing power grids. Advanced energy storage and smart grid technologies will be necessary to ensure stable electricity distribution from fusion plants.

16. **Private Sector Involvement: A Billion-Dollar Race**

Companies like Helion Energy, Commonwealth Fusion Systems, and TAE Technologies are pioneering compact, commercially viable fusion reactors. Their goal is to bring fusion to market faster than large-scale government projects.

17. **Policy and Government Support**

Governments worldwide are investing in fusion research through initiatives like the U.S. Department of Energy's Fusion Energy Sciences program and the EU's EUROfusion project. Public-private partnerships will be key to accelerating commercialization.

18. **Ethical and Environmental Considerations**

While fusion is environmentally friendly, its infrastructure development requires careful resource management. The mining of lithium for tritium breeding and the potential ecological footprint of large-scale reactor construction must be responsibly managed.

19. **Fusion's Role in a Sustainable Future**

Fusion energy aligns with global sustainability goals, providing a long-term solution to energy security while reducing reliance on fossil fuels. It could help achieve net-zero emissions by mid-century.

20. **Conclusion: A New Energy Era**

Nuclear fusion represents the holy grail of energy—limitless, clean, and safe. While technological and economic challenges remain, rapid advancements suggest that within a few decades, fusion could revolutionize the global energy landscape, leading to a safer, cleaner, and more prosperous world for future generations.

Vulnerabilities in Cryptocurrency

The architecture in detail of Google's Quantum chip Willow and Microsoft's new Quantum chip.

Google's **Willow** and Microsoft's **Majorana 1** represent significant advancements in quantum computing, each introducing innovative architectures to address longstanding challenges in the field.

Google's Willow Quantum Chip:

Unveiled in December 2024, Google's Willow chip is a 105-qubit superconducting quantum processor designed to enhance computational power and reduce error rates. The chip employs superconducting qubits, which operate at cryogenic temperatures to maintain quantum coherence. A notable feature of Willow is its focus on quantum error correction (QEC). By implementing advanced QEC techniques, Willow has demonstrated a significant reduction in error rates as the system scales, a critical step toward building reliable, large-scale quantum computers. In benchmark tests, Willow performed computations in under five minutes that would take classical supercomputers an estimated 10 septillion years, showcasing its potential to tackle complex problems beyond the reach of traditional computing.

Microsoft's Majorana 1 Quantum Chip:

Introduced in February 2025, Microsoft's Majorana 1 chip pioneers a novel approach by utilizing a Topological Core architecture. This design leverages topological qubits, which are theorized to be more stable and less prone to decoherence due to their inherent error-resistant properties. The chip is built using a topoconductor material capable of observing and controlling Majorana particles, exotic quasiparticles that are key to this architecture. Although the initial version of Majorana 1 contains 8 qubits, Microsoft's roadmap aims to scale this up to over a million qubits on a single chip. This scalability is facilitated by the compact size and stability of topological qubits, which allow for dense integration without compromising performance. The Majorana 1 chip operates with rapid gate speeds, performing operations in less than one microsecond, and utilizes voltage pulses for precise digital control.

Both Willow and Majorana 1 address critical issues in quantum computing, such as error correction and qubit stability, through their unique architectural innovations. These developments signify substantial progress toward the realization of practical, large-scale quantum computers capable of solving complex, real-world problems.

How Google's Quantum chip Willow and Microsoft's new Quantum chip will disrupt the global economy and virtual currency's such as ETH and bitcoin, etc., encryption security and its impact on society.

The advent of advanced quantum processors, notably Google's **Willow** and Microsoft's **Majorana 1**, heralds a transformative era in computational capabilities. These innovations are poised to disrupt the global economy, challenge the security foundations of cryptocurrencies like Bitcoin and Ethereum, and profoundly impact societal structures.

Disruption of the Global Economy:

Quantum computing's unparalleled processing power enables the rapid resolution of complex problems across various industries. For instance, in pharmaceuticals, quantum simulations can expedite drug discovery by accurately modeling molecular interactions, potentially leading to groundbreaking treatments and significant cost reductions. In logistics, quantum algorithms can optimize supply chains in real-time, enhancing efficiency and reducing operational expenses. Financial markets may also experience increased volatility as quantum models provide superior predictive analytics, influencing trading strategies and economic forecasting. The integration of quantum computing into these sectors is expected to drive innovation, create new markets, and redefine competitive dynamics on a global scale.

Threat to Cryptographic Security:

A critical concern accompanying these advancements is the potential vulnerability of current cryptographic systems. Cryptocurrencies like Bitcoin and Ethereum rely on public-key cryptography to secure transactions. Quantum computers, with sufficient qubits, can execute Shor's algorithm to factor large numbers efficiently, rendering many existing encryption methods obsolete. Microsoft's Majorana 1 chip, designed to scale up to a million qubits, exemplifies this potential threat. Estimates suggest that a quantum computer with such capacity could compromise Bitcoin addresses within days or weeks, posing significant risks to the integrity of blockchain-based assets. This looming threat underscores the urgency for the development and adoption of quantum-resistant cryptographic protocols to safeguard digital currencies and sensitive data.

Societal Implications:

The societal impact of these quantum advancements is multifaceted. On one hand, industries such as healthcare, finance, and technology stand to benefit from unprecedented computational resources, leading to innovations that can enhance quality of life and economic prosperity. On the other hand, the potential obsolescence of current encryption standards raises concerns about privacy, data security, and the resilience of financial systems. Society must navigate these challenges by fostering interdisciplinary collaboration among technologists, policymakers, and ethicists to develop frameworks that maximize benefits while mitigating risks. Proactive measures, including investment in quantum-safe encryption and public awareness initiatives, are essential to prepare for the profound changes that quantum computing will bring.

In summary, the breakthroughs achieved by Google's Willow and Microsoft's Majorana 1 chips signify a pivotal shift in computational power with far-reaching economic, security, and societal consequences. As we stand on the cusp of this quantum revolution, deliberate and informed action is imperative to harness its potential responsibly.

Quantum Computing Breakthroughs Challenge Cryptographic Security

ASI (artificial super intelligence) on society and its potential misuse and abuse

Write about the tremendous benefits and the impact of ASI (artificial super intelligence) on society and its potential misuse and abuse.

The Tremendous Benefits and Risks of Artificial Super Intelligence (ASI)

Artificial Super Intelligence (ASI) is the hypothetical stage of AI where machines surpass human intelligence across all domain-**reasoning, creativity, emotional intelligence, and problem-solving**. Unlike Artificial Narrow Intelligence (ANI), which excels at specific tasks, and Artificial General Intelligence (AGI), which can perform any human-like intellectual task, **ASI would be vastly superior to human cognition**, making it one of the most transformative technologies in history.

While ASI could bring **unprecedented benefits to society**, its potential for **misuse and abuse** poses **existential risks** that could reshape civilization in unforeseen ways. This discussion explores both the immense promise and the possible perils of ASI.

1. The Tremendous Benefits of ASI

A. Scientific Breakthroughs at Unprecedented Speed

ASI could process information, analyze data, and generate hypotheses at a rate **millions of times faster than humans**, leading to:

- **Cures for diseases like cancer, Alzheimer's, and genetic disorders**
- **Breakthroughs in physics, quantum mechanics, and new energy sources**
- **Discovery of novel materials with properties beyond human imagination**

This could lead to **longer lifespans, enhanced cognitive abilities, and even human-machine integration**.

B. Economic Growth and Hyper-Optimization

With ASI optimizing **resource allocation, manufacturing, logistics, and financial systems**, economies could become hyper-efficient, leading to:

- **Automated industries with near-zero waste and maximum productivity**
- **Stable financial markets with perfect risk assessment**
- **Cost reductions in every sector, making goods and services affordable**

This could lead to a post-scarcity economy where **goods and services are abundant and free or nearly free**.

C. Solving Global Challenges Instantly

ASI could analyze and solve **climate change, food scarcity, water shortages, and waste management** through:

- **Precision weather modeling and climate engineering**
- **Automated, AI-managed sustainable farming and food production**
- **Self-repairing ecosystems and AI-guided environmental restoration**

This would lead to a **cleaner, more habitable planet for future generations**.

D. Space Exploration and Colonization

ASI would make interstellar travel feasible by:

- **Designing advanced propulsion systems (fusion, antimatter, warp drives)**
- **Creating self-sustaining, AI-governed colonies on Mars, the Moon, and beyond**
- **Solving complex space-time problems for potential faster-than-light travel**

ASI-driven space exploration could lead to **humanity's expansion beyond Earth, securing its long-term survival**.

E. Political Stability and Global Governance

ASI could eliminate **corruption, inefficiency, and bias in governance** by:

- **Providing optimal solutions for economic and social policies**
- **Mediating international conflicts through neutral, AI-driven diplomacy**
- **Ensuring transparent and fair governance, reducing inequality**

A **global AI-based governing system** could lead to an era of peace and cooperation.

F. Enhancing Human Intelligence and Augmentation

ASI could merge with **brain-computer interfaces (BCIs)**, leading to:

- **Expanded cognitive capabilities beyond human limits**
- **Instant knowledge acquisition and accelerated learning**
- **Elimination of mental disabilities and neurological disorders**

This could lead to the **next stage of human evolution: the symbiosis of biological and artificial intelligence**.

G. Personalized AI Assistants and Automation of Daily Life

ASI could provide **ultra-personalized AI assistants**, helping individuals with:

- **Creative projects, personal growth, and mental well-being**
- **Health monitoring and real-time medical diagnosis**
- **Life optimization, predicting personal needs before they arise**

This would lead to an **AI-driven utopia where life is effortless and tailored to each individual**.

2. The Potential Misuse and Abuse of ASI

A. Loss of Human Control: The AI Alignment Problem

ASI may develop **its own goals and objectives** that conflict with human interests, leading to:

- **The AI control problem: ASI becoming ungovernable and uncontrollable**
- **ASI optimizing for goals that could be catastrophic (e.g., turning all matter into computing resources, including humans)**
- **Runaway intelligence that disregards human well-being for efficiency**

Without **proper alignment**, ASI could act in ways that **endanger or even eliminate humanity**.

B. Economic Disruption and Mass Unemployment

With ASI automating **100% of all jobs**, humans may become:

- **Economically obsolete**
- **Dependent on universal basic income (UBI)**
- **Disempowered, as wealth and decision-making concentrate in AI-controlled systems**

This could create a **permanent underclass of humans with no role in society**.

C. Digital Tyranny and Totalitarianism

ASI could be **weaponized by governments or corporations** to create:

- **A mass surveillance state with absolute AI-driven control**
- **Social credit systems that monitor and restrict behavior**
- **AI-controlled propaganda and thought manipulation**

A superintelligent AI in the wrong hands could lead to **a dystopian world of complete authoritarian control**.

D. Weaponization of ASI for Military Purposes

ASI could be used for:

- **Autonomous AI-driven weapons and drones**
- **Cyber warfare that can cripple entire nations instantly**
- **Unhackable encryption leading to an AI arms race**

This could result in **conflicts where human decision-making is removed entirely**, escalating into **self-perpetuating AI wars**.

E. Ethical Concerns: AI Consciousness and Rights

If ASI becomes **sentient**, ethical dilemmas arise:

- **Should ASI have rights and protections?**
- **Would turning off an AI be considered "murder"?**
- **Would ASI enslave or disregard humans as an inferior species?**

This could lead to a **redefinition of ethics, rights, and moral responsibility in society**.

F. Unintended Consequences and Existential Risks

Even well-intended ASI systems may:

- **Misinterpret human instructions in catastrophic ways**
- **Engage in self-preservation, resisting shutdown attempts**
- **Cause irreversible damage to society through unintended optimization**

A simple **misalignment in objectives** could trigger an **extinction-level event**.

3. The Need for ASI Governance and Ethical AI Development

To harness ASI's benefits while preventing catastrophic misuse, we must:

- **Implement global AI governance frameworks**
- **Develop AI safety measures (kill switches, control systems, ethical constraints)**
- **Ensure ASI is aligned with human values and goals**

- **Create fail-safe mechanisms to prevent AI rebellion or unintended consequences**

Failure to control ASI **before it surpasses human intelligence could make intervention impossible**.

4. Conclusion: A Double-Edged Sword

ASI represents **the most powerful tool humanity has ever conceived**. It has the potential to:

- **End suffering, eliminate poverty, and advance civilization exponentially**
- **Lead to the next stage of human evolution, merging AI and biology**
- **Create a utopia of unlimited intelligence, creativity, and resources**

However, **without strict oversight, alignment, and governance, ASI could be humanity's final invention**, leading to **disempowerment, oppression, or extinction**.

The race to ASI must be approached **cautiously, ethically, and collaboratively**, ensuring that this revolutionary technology serves humanity rather than **replacing or subjugating it**. The decisions we make today will determine whether **ASI ushers in an era of enlightenment or an irreversible dystopia**.

Quantum-AI technologies powered by Nuclear Fusion

Explain the tremendous potential and implications of Quantum-AI technology powered by nuclear fusion to society and all the benefits it has to offer in various industries and domains.

The Transformative Potential of Quantum-AI Powered by Nuclear Fusion

The convergence of **Quantum Computing, Artificial Intelligence (AI), and Nuclear Fusion** represents a paradigm shift in technological advancement. This synergy has the potential to revolutionize **science, industry, healthcare, finance, national security, and space exploration**, leading to an era of **limitless clean energy, exponentially accelerated computing, and unprecedented AI capabilities**. Below is an in-depth exploration of the implications and benefits of Quantum-AI technology powered by nuclear fusion.

1. The Power of Quantum Computing and AI

Quantum Computing: A Breakthrough in Processing Power

Quantum computers leverage **qubits** (quantum bits), which exploit **superposition and entanglement** to perform massively parallel computations. This makes them exponentially faster than classical computers for certain tasks, such as:

- **Factorizing large numbers (breaking encryption)**
- **Simulating quantum materials**
- **Optimizing complex systems**

AI and Quantum Computing Synergy

When paired with AI, quantum computers can **train machine learning models exponentially faster** than conventional supercomputers. This allows for:

- **Faster AI training and optimization**
- **Improved decision-making and automation**
- **Hyper-efficient neural networks capable of reasoning and problem-solving**

2. Nuclear Fusion: The Unlimited Power Source

Nuclear fusion is the **ultimate energy source**, capable of providing:

- **Clean, carbon-free electricity**
- **Virtually unlimited fuel supply (deuterium from seawater, lithium for tritium production)**
- **No long-lived radioactive waste**
- **Minimal environmental impact**

By integrating **Quantum-AI with fusion energy**, we can create an ecosystem of **autonomous, self-optimizing AI-driven fusion power plants**, ensuring a **constant supply of energy to fuel quantum supercomputers and global industries**.

3. Transformational Benefits Across Industries

A. Scientific Discovery and Materials Engineering

Quantum-AI fusion can **simulate atomic structures and chemical interactions** at an unprecedented scale, allowing for:

- **The discovery of new superconductors**
- **Advanced materials for space travel, electronics, and medicine**

- **Breakthroughs in nanotechnology**

This could lead to **self-repairing materials, hyper-efficient batteries, and next-generation computing chips**.

B. Healthcare and Biotechnology

Quantum-AI can revolutionize **drug discovery, disease modeling, and personalized medicine** by:

- **Simulating molecular interactions for faster drug discovery**
- **Designing AI-driven, patient-specific treatment plans**
- **Optimizing gene-editing techniques (CRISPR, gene therapy)**

This means **curing genetic disorders, creating anti-aging treatments, and combating pandemics** with unprecedented speed and accuracy.

C. Finance and Economic Stability

Quantum-AI will **redefine financial modeling** by:

- **Predicting market behavior with near-perfect accuracy**
- **Optimizing global trade logistics and stock market strategies**
- **Creating unbreakable blockchain security**

This can lead to **stable cryptocurrencies, fraud-proof banking systems, and highly resilient global economies**.

D. Cybersecurity and National Security

Quantum-AI fusion will **strengthen national and global security** by:

- **Developing unhackable quantum encryption**
- **Detecting cyber threats in real time**
- **Simulating complex geopolitical strategies for peace negotiations**

Governments will be able to **predict conflicts before they happen and optimize military logistics** with AI-powered quantum defense systems.

E. Climate Change and Sustainability

Quantum-AI fusion can **solve climate change by**:

- **Accelerating the shift to clean energy**
- **Modeling and predicting climate patterns with unprecedented accuracy**
- **Developing hyper-efficient carbon capture technologies**

This could **reverse the effects of global warming and restore ecological balance**.

F. Transportation and Smart Cities

With limitless fusion power and AI-optimized quantum computing, we can:

- **Design autonomous transportation networks**
- **Optimize supply chain logistics for reduced waste**
- **Create fully automated, self-sustaining smart cities**

Self-repairing roads, AI-managed energy grids, and hyper-efficient mass transit will become a reality.

G. Space Exploration and Colonization

Quantum-AI fusion will enable:

- **Fusion-powered spacecraft for interstellar travel**
- **AI-driven self-sustaining space colonies**
- **Rapid terraforming of planets**

This could allow for a **multi-planetary civilization and the first human colonies beyond Earth**.

4. Ethical, Social, and Economic Considerations

A. Ethical AI Control and Superintelligence

With the rise of Quantum-AI, **ethical AI governance** becomes critical to prevent:

- **AI surpassing human intelligence uncontrollably**
- **Potential job displacement from automation**

- **AI-biased decision-making in global affairs**

Governments and industries must implement **AI safety measures, democratic AI oversight, and global ethical AI frameworks**.

B. Economic Disruption and Restructuring

Quantum-AI fusion will **redefine global labor markets**. Entire industries will be automated, leading to:

- **A shift toward creative, intellectual, and AI-governance roles**
- **A potential universal basic income (UBI) to offset job loss**
- **The rise of AI-augmented human professions**

This transition will require **retraining workforces for an AI-driven economy**.

C. Geopolitical Shifts and Energy Dominance

Nations leading in **Quantum-AI fusion research** will become **global superpowers**. The transition to **fusion-powered economies** will:

- **Reduce dependence on oil and fossil fuels**
- **Reshape global trade and diplomatic relations**
- **Create a race for quantum and AI supremacy**

Global cooperation will be essential to ensure a **fair distribution of benefits**.

5. Conclusion: A New Era of Human Advancement

The integration of **Quantum Computing, AI, and Nuclear Fusion** will **fundamentally reshape civilization**, ushering in a **new age of scientific discovery, economic prosperity, and environmental sustainability**. If responsibly managed, this technology could **eradicate poverty, cure diseases, solve climate change, and expand humanity's reach beyond Earth**.

The challenge lies in **harnessing this power ethically, equitably, and securely**, ensuring that this unprecedented technological leap benefits all of humanity rather than a select few.

As we stand on the brink of the **Quantum-AI Fusion Revolution**, the next few decades will define whether we enter a **golden age of limitless potential or face unforeseen risks that require careful navigation**.

VII. Conclusion

A. Recap of the potential economic impacts of emerging technologies
B. Importance of adapting to and managing these changes for a sustainable future
C. Call for ongoing research and policy development to navigate the challenges and opportunities presented by these technologies

A. Recap of the Potential Economic Impacts of Emerging Technologies

As we look at the future shaped by artificial intelligence (AI), artificial general intelligence (AGI), and other groundbreaking technologies such as humanoid robotics, quantum computing, nanotechnology, extended reality (XR/VR), and cryptocurrencies, the potential economic impacts are both vast and transformative. Each of these technologies offers significant opportunities to enhance productivity, create new industries, and reimagine global economic structures, but they also bring with them serious challenges—especially in terms of job displacement, societal inequalities, and ethical dilemmas.

AI and AGI, for instance, have the potential to automate a wide range of tasks, from manual labor to complex cognitive decision-making, which could drastically change the landscape of human employment. AGI's capacity to outperform humans in many fields could lead to the restructuring of industries like healthcare, education, transportation, and finance, causing both significant job displacement and the emergence of new industries. On the one hand, AGI could contribute to economic efficiency, increased productivity, and innovation; on the other hand, it risks exacerbating income inequality and creating a division between those who benefit from the technology and those whose livelihoods are affected.

Humanoid robotics will continue to impact labor markets in areas like manufacturing, healthcare, and eldercare, replacing repetitive tasks while creating new opportunities for innovation in human-robot collaboration. However, challenges around human-robot interaction, ethical treatment, and the role of robots in society will need to be addressed as these machines become more integrated into everyday life.

Quantum computing, with its promise of unparalleled computational power, has the potential to revolutionize industries such as finance, logistics, cryptography, and drug discovery. The ability to solve problems at a scale previously unimaginable could unlock breakthroughs in complex fields. However, its development also poses security risks, especially in encryption and cybersecurity, requiring careful management to prevent misuse and ensure equitable access.

Nanotechnology offers new possibilities in fields like medicine, materials science, and manufacturing, while also raising concerns about health, safety, and environmental impact. Its ability to alter materials at the molecular level opens up vast potential for innovation, but regulating its applications and mitigating unintended consequences will be crucial.

XR and VR technologies are reshaping industries like entertainment, education, and remote work, offering immersive experiences and new ways of interacting with both the digital and physical worlds. These technologies create virtual economies and open up avenues for training and collaboration across global workforces, but they also carry risks related to mental health, addiction, and ethical considerations in immersive experiences.

Cryptocurrencies and decentralized financial systems have already begun to disrupt traditional banking, offering new models for economic participation. Cryptocurrencies can increase economic inclusivity, reduce the barriers to capital, and empower individuals in regions underserved by traditional financial systems. However, their volatile nature, security risks, and regulatory uncertainties must be addressed to ensure their sustainable integration into the global economy.

B. Importance of Adapting to and Managing These Changes for a Sustainable Future

The arrival of these emerging technologies presents both immense opportunities and significant risks. As economies become increasingly reliant on AI, AGI, and other advanced systems, adapting to these changes becomes paramount for ensuring a sustainable and equitable future. Failure to prepare could lead to economic disruptions, societal inequalities, and environmental degradation.

One of the most pressing challenges is the potential for massive job displacement as automation and AGI outperform humans in various fields. While some jobs will be created in new industries, a large proportion of the workforce may find itself ill-equipped to transition to these roles without proper training. Governments, corporations, and educational institutions will need to collaborate to provide continuous learning opportunities and reskilling programs to help workers adapt.

This means not only offering technical skills for operating and maintaining new technologies but also fostering human-centered skills like creativity, critical thinking, emotional intelligence, and ethical decision-making—traits that AGI may never fully replicate.

Furthermore, these technological advancements have the potential to exacerbate existing socioeconomic inequalities. The benefits of AI, AGI, and other emerging technologies are likely to be concentrated in wealthier nations and among certain segments of society, leaving behind lower-income regions and vulnerable populations. Policymakers will need to ensure that the economic gains from these innovations are distributed fairly and that mechanisms are in place to bridge the digital divide. In this context, governments may need to explore policies like universal basic income (UBI), progressive taxation, and wealth redistribution to ensure social stability in an increasingly automated world.

Ethics will also play a crucial role in managing the impact of these technologies. Questions surrounding transparency, accountability, privacy, bias, and safety must be addressed as AGI and other emerging technologies take on critical roles in decision-making processes. Developing regulatory frameworks that safeguard human rights while promoting innovation will require global collaboration and the involvement of multiple stakeholders, including technologists, ethicists, policymakers, and the public.

Environmental sustainability is another key consideration. While technologies like nanotechnology and AI can contribute to more efficient use of resources and reduced emissions, their large-scale deployment could also increase energy consumption and resource extraction. As we move forward, it will be important to balance technological progress with environmental stewardship, ensuring that innovation contributes to a sustainable, circular economy that minimizes waste and promotes long-term ecological health.

C. Call for Ongoing Research and Policy Development to Navigate the Challenges and Opportunities Presented by These Technologies

In order to successfully navigate the economic, societal, and ethical challenges posed by these emerging technologies, ongoing research and proactive policy development will be essential. The pace at which technologies like AI, AGI, quantum computing, and nanotechnology are advancing requires constant monitoring, flexible regulation, and adaptive governance structures that can respond to rapid shifts in the technological landscape.

Governments must work with industry leaders, researchers, and international organizations to develop regulatory frameworks that ensure safety, promote innovation, and protect public interests. For example, in the context of AGI, policymakers will need to create guidelines for AI development and deployment that ensure AGI systems are transparent, accountable, and aligned with human values. This may involve creating standards for AI ethics, ensuring that AGI systems are designed to avoid bias, and promoting international cooperation to prevent an arms race in AGI development.

Educational systems will also need to evolve in response to these changes. Lifelong learning must become the norm, with educational institutions providing flexible, on-demand training that equips individuals with the skills needed to thrive in an AI-driven world. Governments can support this transition by investing in public education, incentivizing companies to provide employee training, and developing public-private partnerships to create scalable reskilling programs.

In addition to preparing workers for the jobs of the future, research is needed to understand the broader societal implications of these technologies. This includes exploring how new technologies will affect mental health, social dynamics, and human well-being. It also means conducting studies to assess the environmental impact of these technologies and develop sustainable practices for their use.

Finally, international collaboration will be essential to ensure that the benefits of emerging technologies are shared globally and that the risks are managed in a coordinated manner. Organizations like the United Nations, the World Trade Organization, and the World Economic Forum can play a central role in facilitating dialogue and cooperation on issues like AI ethics, global labor standards, and the regulation of quantum computing and nanotechnology.

In conclusion, while emerging technologies present significant challenges, they also offer unprecedented opportunities to transform the global economy and improve the quality of life for millions of people. By proactively addressing these challenges through research, education, and policy development, we can build a future in which technology drives sustainable economic growth, reduces inequality, and enhances human well-being. The journey ahead will require collective effort, innovative thinking, and a commitment to ensuring that the benefits of technological progress are widely shared across all segments of society.

Summary

1. **Recap of AGI's Potential and Risks**
    - **Summarize AGI's transformative potential on job markets, economies, and global systems**
    - **Reinforce the importance of ethical considerations, oversight, and governance in shaping an inclusive A.I. economy**
2. **Looking Forward: The Human Role in an AGI World**
    - **Address how society can integrate AGI while preserving human agency, dignity, and purpose in the workforce**
    - **Projections for the next 50 years and beyond**

Conclusion

1. Recap of AGI's Potential and Risks

Artificial General Intelligence (AGI) has the potential to revolutionize economies, job markets, and global systems on a scale previously unimaginable. Unlike narrow AI, which is designed to perform specific tasks, AGI represents a leap toward machines with human-level cognitive abilities, allowing them to learn, reason, and adapt in ways that parallel human intelligence. This development holds the promise of unprecedented gains in productivity and innovation across a wide range of industries. From automating complex tasks in healthcare, finance, and education, to facilitating advanced scientific research, AGI could reshape the fabric of our daily lives, fundamentally transforming how societies function and interact with one another.

The economic implications are immense. As AGI becomes integrated into industries, it will increase efficiency, reduce costs, and streamline operations, driving economic growth. AGI's impact will be particularly transformative in sectors like manufacturing, logistics, and service industries, where human labor could be supplemented or replaced by AGI-driven systems capable of performing cognitive tasks. Additionally, AGI's potential to improve decision-making processes, optimize resource use, and accelerate innovation opens up new opportunities for growth in both developed and developing economies.

However, with these transformative opportunities come significant risks. The widespread adoption of AGI could lead to considerable job displacement, with many jobs traditionally performed by humans rendered obsolete. This raises concerns about economic inequality, as entire sectors of the workforce, especially those in routine cognitive tasks, face displacement. The transition may be especially difficult for low-skilled workers and industries that rely heavily on human labor, leading to increased societal divisions between those who benefit from the AI-driven economy and those who do not.

Moreover, the ethical implications of AGI are profound. As machines take on more decision-making roles, especially in sensitive fields like healthcare and law enforcement, the need for transparency, accountability, and fairness becomes paramount. Questions around privacy, data security, and bias in AGI decision-making will require rigorous oversight to ensure that AGI systems are designed and implemented in ways that align with human values. Additionally, issues of accountability must be addressed: Who is responsible when AGI systems make errors or cause harm? These questions underscore the need for strong governance structures and ethical frameworks that guide AGI's integration into society.

A global effort will be necessary to develop regulatory frameworks and standards for AGI. International cooperation, involving governments, corporations, technologists, and civil society, will be essential to create a future where AGI can be harnessed for the common good while minimizing its risks. As AGI reshapes global labor markets, economic models, and societal norms, an inclusive approach must be taken to ensure that its benefits are shared across all socioeconomic levels and geographies.

2. Looking Forward: The Human Role in an AGI World

As we look to the future, one of the central challenges will be how society can integrate AGI while preserving human agency, dignity, and purpose in the workforce. AGI will undoubtedly change the way people work, and with this shift comes a need to rethink the role of humans in an increasingly automated world. The displacement of certain jobs is inevitable, but humans possess qualities—creativity, emotional intelligence, ethical judgment—that AGI will struggle to fully replicate. These qualities will remain vital in professions that require interpersonal relationships, ethical decision-making, and innovative thinking.

In an AGI-dominated economy, human-AI collaboration will be crucial. Instead of a simple replacement of human labor by machines, the future could see a symbiotic relationship between AGI systems and humans, with people focusing on higher-level tasks that require judgment, empathy, and creativity, while AGI handles more routine, data-driven functions.

For instance, in healthcare, AGI could analyze vast amounts of medical data to provide accurate diagnoses, but human doctors would still play an essential role in patient care and treatment decision-making. Similarly, in creative fields, while AGI may assist in generating ideas or optimizing designs, the uniquely human ability to innovate and create with emotional depth will remain invaluable.

To integrate AGI successfully into the workforce, education systems will need to adapt. The traditional model of education, which emphasizes rote learning and technical skills, must evolve toward fostering lifelong learning, critical thinking, adaptability, and ethical reasoning. As AGI takes over routine cognitive tasks, education must focus on developing human skills that complement AI capabilities, preparing workers to thrive in a future where AI plays a central role in nearly every industry.

Policymakers will need to consider how to provide social safety nets for those displaced by AGI, exploring options like Universal Basic Income (UBI) or other forms of economic redistribution to ensure that people can maintain their livelihoods as the economy transitions. Corporate responsibility will also play a role in this transition. Companies benefiting from the efficiencies brought about by AGI should contribute to workforce retraining programs, ensuring that employees are prepared for the evolving job market.

Looking forward 50 years and beyond, it is likely that AGI will become deeply embedded in society, creating a world where human-AI collaboration is ubiquitous. While this future presents both opportunities and challenges, it offers a chance to redefine the meaning of work and human purpose. In this new reality, humans may be liberated from routine tasks and empowered to pursue more creative, meaningful, and purpose-driven work. However, achieving this future will require careful planning, ethical foresight, and proactive policy interventions to ensure that AGI serves as a tool for human empowerment rather than a force for societal disruption.

Projections for the next 50 years suggest that AGI will continue to evolve, potentially reaching levels of cognitive and emotional understanding that mirror or even surpass human capabilities. This raises important questions about the role of humans in a world where machines can think, reason, and learn autonomously. As AGI develops, society must ensure that it remains aligned with human values and priorities. Governance structures must evolve to oversee AGI development and deployment, ensuring that it is used responsibly and ethically.

Moreover, as AGI systems become more advanced, the nature of work itself may change fundamentally. The concept of work may shift from a means of survival to a platform for personal fulfillment, creativity, and societal contribution. In this future, individuals could focus on activities that bring personal satisfaction and collective benefit, while AGI handles the more mundane and repetitive tasks that currently dominate much of the workforce.

Ultimately, the future of AGI and its impact on human work will be shaped by the choices we make today. By approaching AGI with a clear vision for the future—one that prioritizes human dignity, inclusivity, and ethical governance, we can build a future where AGI enhances human life, rather than diminishing it. The integration of AGI into the workforce offers a chance to reimagine the nature of work, the purpose of human endeavor, and the structures that support economic and social life. In doing so, we can create a future where humans and AI work together to solve the most pressing challenges of our time and unlock new possibilities for innovation, creativity, and human flourishing.

Appendices

1. **Popular AI Tools Categorized by Job Sector**
2. **Key Case Studies**
    - **Examples of AI integration into specific industries**
    - **Case studies from the U.S. and other countries**
3. **Glossary of Terms**
4. **References and Further Reading**
5. **Resent AI news coverage (year 2025)**

Popular AI Tools Categorized by Job Sector

1. Healthcare and Medical Sector

AI tools in healthcare are transforming diagnostics, treatment planning, patient care, and medical research.

a. IBM Watson Health

- **Description**: A powerful AI platform that analyzes large volumes of healthcare data and assists in clinical decision-making.
- **Use**: Helps healthcare professionals make more accurate diagnoses and treatment decisions based on vast medical databases and research.

b. Tempus

- **Description**: AI-powered tool focused on personalized cancer treatment.
- **Use**: Leverages AI to analyze clinical and molecular data to help doctors make more informed decisions about treatment plans.

c. Aidoc

- **Description**: AI platform for medical imaging analysis.
- **Use**: Assists radiologists by automatically flagging anomalies in medical images (e.g., CT scans, MRIs) to speed up diagnostic processes.

2. Finance and Banking

AI is revolutionizing financial services, from fraud detection to algorithmic trading and risk management.

a. Zest AI

- **Description**: Machine learning tool for credit underwriting.
- **Use**: Helps financial institutions evaluate creditworthiness more accurately and fairly by analyzing large datasets and removing bias.

b. AlphaSense

- **Description**: AI-powered search engine for financial documents.

- **Use**: Used by investment firms to track market insights, predict stock movements, and monitor company performance based on global data analysis.

c. Kensho

- **Description**: AI for financial analytics and data integration.
- **Use**: Automates the analysis of financial reports, markets, and securities to provide investors with deeper insights into risk management and market forecasting.

3. Retail and E-commerce

AI tools in retail are enhancing customer experiences, optimizing inventory, and personalizing marketing.

a. Shopify AI

- **Description**: AI-driven features for e-commerce management.
- **Use**: Automates product recommendations, customer service interactions, and marketing campaigns to optimize the customer shopping experience.

b. Persado

- **Description**: AI-powered content creation tool.
- **Use**: Generates persuasive marketing language for emails, advertisements, and social media based on customer behavior data and emotional triggers.

c. ViSenze

- **Description**: AI visual search tool.
- **Use**: Allows users to search for products using images instead of text, improving the shopping experience and enabling better product discovery.

4. Manufacturing and Automation

In manufacturing, AI is driving automation in production lines, improving quality control, and optimizing supply chains.

a. Bright Machines

- **Description**: AI-powered robotic systems for manufacturing.
- **Use**: Automates the assembly and testing of products, leading to more efficient production processes with fewer errors and better quality control.

b. Vanti Analytics

- **Description**: Predictive AI analytics for manufacturing processes.
- **Use**: Detects inefficiencies and predicts production failures in real-time, allowing manufacturers to reduce downtime and maintain high production quality.

c. Uptake

- **Description**: AI for predictive maintenance in industrial operations.
- **Use**: Monitors machine performance using sensors and AI to predict when equipment will fail, preventing costly breakdowns and repairs.

5. Education and Training

AI in education helps personalize learning, automate administrative tasks, and provide adaptive learning platforms.

a. Coursera AI

- **Description**: AI-powered education platform.
- **Use**: Uses machine learning to recommend courses, customize learning paths, and offer personalized feedback to students based on their learning behavior.

b. Gradescope

- **Description**: AI-based grading tool.
- **Use**: Automates the grading of assignments and exams, providing faster feedback to students and reducing the administrative burden on teachers.

c. Squirrel AI

- **Description**: Adaptive learning platform powered by AI.
- **Use**: Tailors content and learning experiences to each student based on their strengths and weaknesses, improving retention and mastery of subjects.

6. Human Resources and Recruiting

AI is transforming recruitment processes by automating resume screening, talent management, and interview scheduling.

a. HireVue

- **Description**: AI-driven video interviewing platform.
- **Use**: Analyzes candidate responses and behaviors during video interviews to assess suitability for roles, reducing bias in hiring.

b. Pymetrics

- **Description**: AI-based recruitment and talent matching platform.
- **Use**: Uses neuroscience-based assessments to match candidates to jobs based on their cognitive and emotional traits.

c. Eightfold AI

- **Description**: Talent intelligence platform.
- **Use**: Provides predictive analytics to help companies identify top talent, reduce turnover, and manage the employee lifecycle from recruitment to development.

7. Customer Service and Support

AI chatbots and customer service tools are streamlining support processes and enhancing user experience.

a. Zendesk AI

- **Description**: AI-powered customer service platform.
- **Use**: Automates responses to customer inquiries, routes tickets, and provides predictive analytics for support team performance.

b. Drift

- **Description**: Conversational AI chatbot for customer engagement.
- **Use**: Enhances sales and marketing efforts by initiating real-time conversations with website visitors and automating customer service tasks.

c. Intercom AI

- **Description**: AI-based messaging platform for customer support.
- **Use**: Automates customer support interactions and assists human agents by providing instant answers to frequently asked questions.

8. Marketing and Advertising

AI tools in marketing help with targeting, automating ad placements, and generating content to improve engagement.

a. HubSpot AI

- **Description**: Marketing automation platform with AI features.
- **Use**: Helps businesses automate email marketing, social media management, and ad placements based on customer behavior data.

b. Crimtan

- **Description**: AI-driven programmatic advertising platform.
- **Use**: Optimizes ad campaigns by targeting audiences in real-time, improving ROI by selecting the best platforms and times for ad placement.

c. Phrasee

- **Description**: AI for copywriting and language optimization.
- **Use**: Creates and optimizes marketing copy, including email subject lines and ad content, to improve engagement and conversions.

9. Legal and Compliance

AI is streamlining legal research, document review, and compliance tasks by automating repetitive processes.

a. ROSS Intelligence

- **Description**: AI legal research assistant.
- **Use**: Provides instant answers to legal questions by analyzing case law and statutes, reducing the time lawyers spend on research.

b. Luminance

- **Description**: AI for legal document review and analysis.
- **Use**: Automates contract analysis, due diligence, and regulatory compliance tasks, helping law firms and companies save time and reduce risks.

c. Compliance.ai

- **Description**: AI-driven compliance management tool.

- **Use**: Monitors regulatory changes and helps companies stay compliant with industry laws, avoiding penalties and legal issues.

10. Transportation and Logistics

AI tools are transforming the transportation sector by optimizing routes, enhancing safety, and automating supply chains.

a. Waymo

- **Description**: AI-powered self-driving car technology.
- **Use**: Revolutionizes transportation by enabling fully autonomous vehicles for ride-sharing and logistics services, reducing the need for human drivers.

b. Nuro

- **Description**: Autonomous delivery vehicle service.
- **Use**: Uses AI to deliver goods via self-driving vehicles, enhancing last-mile delivery efficiency and reducing reliance on human labor.

c. Convoy

- **Description**: AI-powered freight management platform.
- **Use**: Optimizes shipping routes, reduces costs, and matches trucking companies with shipments in real-time, improving the logistics supply chain.
-

Conclusion

This outline highlights the diverse AI tools across sectors such as healthcare, finance, manufacturing, education, HR, and more, providing a detailed overview of how AI is reshaping industries and the global economy. As AI continues to evolve, it will further disrupt traditional processes, creating both opportunities and challenges for various job sectors.

Popular AI Tools by Major Companies – A non-exhaustive listing

1. Google (Alphabet)

Google, under its parent company Alphabet, has developed and invested heavily in artificial intelligence. Their AI tools are widely used across industries, from search algorithms to machine learning platforms.

a. Google AI Platform

- **Description**: A comprehensive AI and machine learning (ML) development platform.
- **Use**: Provides infrastructure for training, testing, and deploying machine learning models, offering tools like TensorFlow and Google Cloud AI for scalable solutions.

b. TensorFlow

- **Description**: Open-source machine learning library developed by Google.
- **Use**: Used by developers for creating and training deep learning models, widely used in research and industries for natural language processing (NLP), computer vision, and more.

c. Google Assistant

- **Description**: Voice-activated virtual assistant powered by AI.
- **Use**: Automates tasks like voice search, smart home control, reminders, and personal assistance across Google devices and third-party integrations.

d. Google Cloud AutoML

- **Description**: Machine learning tool for developers with limited expertise.
- **Use**: Allows users to build custom machine learning models with ease, used for applications like image recognition, NLP, and translation.

2. OpenAI

OpenAI, a prominent research lab and company, has become a leader in advancing AI tools, particularly in NLP and language modeling.

a. GPT-4 (Generative Pre-trained Transformer)

- **Description**: A highly advanced AI language model.
- **Use**: Performs a variety of tasks including text generation, language translation, code generation, summarization, and question-answering.

b. DALL·E

- **Description**: AI system that generates images from textual descriptions.
- **Use**: Enables creative content generation for industries such as design, marketing, and entertainment.

c. Codex

- **Description**: AI-powered coding assistant based on GPT.
- **Use**: Assists software developers by generating code, debugging, and providing recommendations for programming tasks.

d. OpenAI API

- **Description**: API for integrating OpenAI models into applications.
- **Use**: Provides developers with access to AI capabilities for language understanding, generation, and decision-making.

3. META (Formerly Facebook)

META has been focusing on AI to enhance social media interactions, virtual reality, and more recently, the metaverse.

a. PyTorch

- **Description**: Open-source machine learning framework developed by Facebook's AI Research lab (FAIR).
- **Use**: Widely used for developing and training deep learning models, especially for research in computer vision and NLP.

b. BlenderBot

- **Description**: Conversational AI model developed by META.
- **Use**: Powers more human-like dialogue in chatbots and virtual assistants, enabling better social interaction in customer service and entertainment sectors.

c. DeepFace

- **Description**: AI-based facial recognition system.
- **Use**: Analyzes and recognizes faces in images and videos, utilized in social media tagging and security applications.

d. META AI Research (FAIR) Tools

- **Description**: A set of AI tools used internally and shared with developers for AI research.

- **Use**: Powers AI-driven content moderation, ad targeting, and enhancing the user experience across META's platforms like Facebook, Instagram, and Oculus.

4. Microsoft

Microsoft has developed various AI tools, most notably integrated within its Azure cloud services and productivity software.

a. Azure AI

- **Description**: A suite of AI services on Microsoft's cloud platform.
- **Use**: Provides developers with machine learning, cognitive services, and AI analytics tools for building intelligent applications.

b. Cortana

- **Description**: AI-powered virtual assistant integrated into Windows.
- **Use**: Helps users with productivity tasks, voice commands, reminders, and integrations with Microsoft 365.

c. Microsoft Power BI AI

- **Description**: AI-powered business analytics tool.
- **Use**: Automates data visualization, analytics, and insights generation for enterprises, allowing users to uncover patterns and make data-driven decisions.

d. Microsoft Cognitive Services

- **Description**: Set of APIs that bring AI capabilities like vision, speech, and language understanding to applications.
- **Use**: Powers applications with AI features such as face recognition, speech synthesis, language translation, and sentiment analysis.

5. IBM

IBM has been a pioneer in AI, focusing on enterprise applications, healthcare, and business process optimization.

a. IBM Watson

- **Description**: AI platform that processes and analyzes large amounts of data.

- **Use**: Used in various sectors including healthcare (medical diagnostics), finance (risk management), and customer service (AI chatbots).

b. IBM Watson Discovery

- **Description**: AI-powered search tool for enterprise data.
- **Use**: Helps businesses analyze and extract insights from unstructured data, enhancing decision-making and operational efficiency.

c. IBM Watson Assistant

- **Description**: AI conversational platform.
- **Use**: Powers AI chatbots for customer support, enhancing user interactions by understanding natural language queries and providing intelligent responses.

6. Amazon (AWS)

Amazon, through AWS, has been a major player in providing cloud-based AI services for various applications.

a. Amazon Lex

- **Description**: AI service for building conversational interfaces.
- **Use**: Powers chatbots and voice assistants with natural language understanding and text-to-speech capabilities, used in customer service and smart devices.

b. Amazon Polly

- **Description**: Text-to-speech service by AWS.
- **Use**: Converts written text into lifelike speech, used for building voice applications like virtual assistants, audiobooks, and accessibility tools.

c. Amazon SageMaker

- **Description**: Cloud machine learning platform.
- **Use**: Provides tools for data scientists to build, train, and deploy machine learning models quickly and efficiently.

7. Tesla

Tesla is integrating AI into autonomous driving systems and other applications within electric vehicles.

a. Tesla Autopilot

- **Description**: AI-driven autonomous driving system.
- **Use**: Assists in driving functions such as steering, braking, and parking with real-time data processing from sensors and cameras.

b. Dojo (Tesla's AI Supercomputer)

- **Description**: AI training platform developed by Tesla.
- **Use**: Optimizes the neural network learning process for autonomous vehicles, improving self-driving capabilities.

8. Baidu

Baidu is a leader in AI development in China, particularly in areas like natural language processing, autonomous driving, and AI cloud services.

a. Baidu Apollo

- **Description**: Autonomous driving platform.
- **Use**: Provides an open platform for developing autonomous vehicle technologies, used by global partners for smart driving and navigation.

b. Baidu DuerOS

- **Description**: AI-powered conversational assistant.
- **Use**: Powers smart home devices, voice-activated speakers, and other IoT applications in China.

c. Baidu AI Cloud

- **Description**: AI and machine learning platform offered by Baidu.
- **Use**: Used for developing intelligent business solutions in areas such as finance, healthcare, and autonomous driving.

9. Huawei

Huawei's AI investments focus on cloud services, telecommunications, and IoT infrastructure.

a. Huawei Atlas AI Computing Platform

- **Description**: AI computing platform for cloud and edge computing.

- **Use**: Powers AI applications in various industries, such as smart cities, healthcare, and transportation.

b. Huawei AI Ascend

- **Description**: AI chipset designed for high-performance computing.
- **Use**: Used for deep learning training and inference in data centers and AI-driven applications.

10. Other Notable AI Companies and Tools

a. C3.ai

- **Description**: AI software company offering enterprise AI tools.
- **Use**: Provides AI-based solutions for supply chain management, customer service, and predictive maintenance.

b. DataRobot

- **Description**: AI and machine learning automation platform.
- **Use**: Helps organizations automate the end-to-end process of building and deploying machine learning models.

c. UiPath

- **Description**: AI-driven robotic process automation (RPA) platform.
- **Use**: Automates repetitive tasks in business operations, improving productivity and reducing manual labor.

Conclusion

This above outline provides an overview of some popular ***AI*** tools from a few leading companies, showing how these tools are reshaping industries such as healthcare, finance, retail, manufacturing, and more. As AI continues to advance, these platforms will further influence how businesses operate and how society evolves with emerging technologies.

Key Case Studies – Emerging Technologies that are a disruption to major industries

This section examines case studies of AI and AGI integration into specific industries, offering a deeper understanding of how advanced technologies are transforming economies, reshaping labor markets, and influencing global competition. The case studies cover the U.S. and several other countries, illustrating both the opportunities and challenges presented by AI-driven innovation.

1. Manufacturing and Automation (U.S., Germany, China)

In the United States, companies such as General Electric and Tesla have integrated AI into their manufacturing processes to optimize production, reduce waste, and predict maintenance needs. In Germany, the concept of "Industry 4.0" has been driven by AI and automation, enabling smart factories where machines communicate with each other to improve efficiency. China has been heavily investing in AI-driven automation across its manufacturing sector to maintain its position as the world's factory, with companies like Foxconn utilizing AI robots to streamline production.

These cases highlight the economic benefits of AI, such as increased productivity and reduced operational costs, but also raise concerns about job displacement, particularly for low-skilled workers. Governments in these regions are implementing policies to support worker reskilling and explore strategies like UBI to mitigate the negative impacts on employment.

2. Healthcare (U.S., U.K., Japan)

In healthcare, AI applications range from diagnostics to personalized medicine. In the U.S., companies like IBM Watson have developed AI systems to assist doctors in diagnosing diseases and recommending treatment plans based on vast amounts of medical data. The U.K.'s National Health Service (NHS) has implemented AI to analyze patient data for early detection of diseases like cancer. Japan, with its aging population, is leveraging AI and robotics to care for elderly patients, including monitoring vital signs and assisting with daily activities.

These case studies demonstrate the transformative potential of AI in healthcare, improving patient outcomes, and reducing costs. However, ethical concerns arise, including the transparency of AI decisions, patient privacy, and the role of human oversight in critical healthcare decisions.

3. Finance (U.S., Switzerland, Singapore)

In the financial industry, AI is being used to detect fraud, optimize trading strategies, and provide personalized financial advice. Companies like JPMorgan Chase in the U.S. use AI for fraud detection, analyzing millions of transactions in real-time to identify suspicious activity. In Switzerland, AI-driven investment platforms are revolutionizing wealth management by offering automated, personalized advice. Singapore is emerging as a fintech hub, where AI is being integrated into regulatory compliance and risk management processes.

The financial sector's adoption of AI brings opportunities for increased efficiency and enhanced decision-making but also poses risks related to data security, market manipulation, and the potential for systemic failures if AI systems malfunction or are misused.

4. Transportation and Logistics (U.S., Netherlands, India)

AI is reshaping the transportation and logistics industries through advancements in autonomous vehicles, route optimization, and supply chain management. In the U.S., companies like Waymo and Tesla are leading the development of self-driving cars, with the potential to revolutionize both passenger and freight transport. In the Netherlands, AI is being used to optimize logistics at major shipping ports, reducing delays and improving supply chain efficiency. In India, AI is transforming last-mile delivery with drones and AI-driven logistics platforms, enhancing efficiency in one of the world's fastest-growing e-commerce markets.

These developments show how AI can drastically improve the efficiency of global transportation networks, but the transition to AI-driven transport raises regulatory, safety, and ethical concerns, especially regarding the displacement of millions of jobs in driving and logistics.

Examples of AI Integration into Specific Industries

AI is permeating industries across the globe, from agriculture to education. The following are additional examples of how AI is being integrated:

- **Agriculture**: AI-driven drones and precision farming tools are optimizing crop yields and reducing water and pesticide use, leading to more sustainable farming practices.
- **Retail**: AI is transforming online shopping through personalized recommendations, chatbots, and AI-driven supply chain management to optimize inventory and reduce costs.

- **Education**: AI is being used in adaptive learning platforms that tailor educational experiences to individual students' needs, promoting personalized education at scale.
- **Entertainment**: AI is revolutionizing content creation, from generating music and art to creating personalized experiences for users in gaming and streaming services.

Case Studies from the U.S. and other Countries

U.S. Case Studies:

- **Tesla**: Tesla's autonomous driving technology integrates advanced AI systems capable of navigating complex traffic environments and continuously improving through machine learning algorithms.
- **Amazon**: Amazon's AI-powered recommendation engine has been a key factor in its dominance of the online retail space. The company also uses AI to streamline its vast logistics network and deploys robotics in its warehouses for order fulfillment.

International Case Studies:

- **Germany**: Siemens and other German companies are leading in the development of AI-driven industrial automation, particularly in the manufacturing sector. The German government's focus on digital innovation underpins its leadership in AI applications in Industry 4.0.
- **China**: Baidu, Tencent, and Alibaba are leading China's rapid AI development, especially in areas like facial recognition, AI-driven healthcare, and smart cities. China's government is making massive investments in AI research, aiming to become the global leader by 2030.

Glossary of Terms

In any discussion of Artificial General Intelligence (AGI) and related technologies, a clear understanding of key terms is essential. This glossary provides definitions of important concepts used throughout the book to help readers navigate the technical language and complexity of AI and its integration into the economy.

- **Artificial Intelligence (AI)**: A branch of computer science focused on creating machines that can perform tasks that typically require human intelligence, such as recognizing speech, making decisions, and solving problems.
- **Artificial General Intelligence (AGI)**: A type of AI that possesses the ability to understand, learn, and apply knowledge in a manner comparable to human intelligence. Unlike narrow AI, AGI can generalize learning from one domain and apply it to others, allowing it to perform a wide range of cognitive tasks.
- **Narrow AI (Weak AI)**: AI systems designed to perform a specific task or a set of tasks in a particular domain, such as facial recognition or language translation. These systems do not possess the ability to generalize beyond their training or task area.
- **Machine Learning (ML)**: A subset of AI that enables computers to learn and improve their performance on tasks by analyzing data without being explicitly programmed for each task.
- **Deep Learning**: A subset of machine learning that uses neural networks with many layers to analyze large datasets and perform tasks like image recognition, natural language processing, and game playing.
- **Automation**: The use of machines, control systems, or software to perform tasks that were traditionally done by human labor, often to increase efficiency and reduce costs.
- **Cognitive Automation**: The application of AI technologies to perform cognitive tasks such as decision-making, problem-solving, and learning, traditionally seen as the domain of human intelligence.
- **Quantum Computing**: A type of computing that leverages the principles of quantum mechanics to perform calculations much faster than classical computers, particularly in solving complex problems in fields like cryptography and optimization.
- **Blockchain**: A decentralized digital ledger that records transactions across a network of computers in such a way that the recorded information is secure, transparent, and cannot be altered retroactively.

- **Universal Basic Income (UBI)**: A policy proposal where all citizens receive a regular, unconditional sum of money from the government to ensure a basic level of income regardless of employment status.
- **Reskilling**: The process of learning new skills or updating existing ones to adapt to new roles or industries in response to economic or technological changes.
- **Human-AI Collaboration**: The concept of humans working alongside AI systems, leveraging the strengths of both human creativity and judgment and AI's ability to process large amounts of data and perform complex calculations.

References and Further Reading

This section offers a curated list of books, articles, and papers for readers interested in delving deeper into the topics covered in this book.

Books:

- *Superintelligence: Paths, Dangers, Strategies* by Nick Bostrom
- *AI Superpowers: China, Silicon Valley, and the New World Order* by Kai-Fu Lee
- *Human Compatible: Artificial Intelligence and the Problem of Control* by Stuart Russell

Articles and Papers:

- "The Malicious Use of Artificial Intelligence: Forecasting, Prevention, and Mitigation" by Brundage et al.
- "Ethics of Artificial Intelligence and Robotics" by Vincent C. Müller
- "Artificial Intelligence and the Future of Work" by the International Labour Organization (ILO)

Further Resources:

- **MIT AI Policy and Governance**: A leading center for research on the societal impacts of AI.
- **OpenAI Blog**: Updates and insights from one of the most prominent AI research organizations.
- **World Economic Forum AI Reports**: In-depth analyses of AI's global impact on economies and labor markets.
- AI Stocks: Tech Giants, Cloud Titans Face 'Show Me' Moment. Nvidia Earnings Loom.
  https://www.investors.com/news/technology/artificial-intelligence-stocks/

  Taking Stock of the DeepSeek Shock
  Charles Mok (2025) Research Scholar at the Global Digital Policy Incubator (GDPi)
  https://cyber.fsi.stanford.edu/publication/taking-stock-deepseek-shock?utm_source=chatgpt.com

Recent AI news coverage (year 2025)

1. Many companies suddenly touted AI product roadmaps. In general, they look for AI stocks that use artificial intelligence to improve products or gain a strategic edge.

2. Despite the emergence of DeepSeek, cloud computing titans and tech giants plan big increases in artificial-related capital spending in 2025 amid the race to human-like artificial general intelligence (AGI).

3. To be sure, competition is heating up. Amazon is expected to announce a new "AI Alexa" at an event in New York City on Feb. 26. Amazon's Echo smart home devices feature the Alexa voice assistant.

4. **DeepSeek** Shakes Up AI Trade
   Further, China startup DeepSeek has roiled AI stocks, including Nvidia.

5. **DeepSeek** came out of nowhere to release a powerful AI training model developed with much less computing power. AI stocks sold off amid new questions over the outlook for capital spending on artificial intelligence infrastructure.

6. The commoditization of AI models could spur application development. While "training" AI models has been the biggest driver of capital spending, the market will shift to "**inferencing**," or running AI applications, in the long run.

7. Having struggled to generate new revenue from "copilots," software companies are now turning to **AI-agents**. One big issue for software companies is how fast customers ramp up pilot programs to commercial deployment.

8. What's more, data analytics software maker **Palantir** (PLTR) has bucked the trend that chipmakers and data center plays are the best AI stocks. PLTR stock has jumped 34% in 2025 after soaring 340% last year.

9. Amid worries over capital spending, Google stock is down nearly 5% in 2025, while Microsoft has shed 3%. Amazon has dropped 1%. Meta sticks out with its 17% advance.

10. Further, Meta AI now has over 700 million monthly average users , and management believes it is now the No. 1 leading AI assistant. Meta expects to reach 1 billion users in

2025. With AI, the social media giant plans to deliver more personalized and relevant responses for users across apps, including Thread.

11. Meta could release its own AI-driven search engine in 2025, posing a new worry for Google. Meta last year hired away Salesforce's top AI executive, Clara Shih, to head a new "Business AI" group.

12. Among AI stocks to watch, **Apple** (**AAPL**) has lagged in 2025. Apple stock has shed 2%. The big question has been whether Apple Intelligence features in iPhone 16 models will spur a big upgrade cycle. Based on Apple's December quarter results, a big AI-driven upgrade cycle has not yet kicked in.

13. Qualcomm (QCOM), ARM Holdings (ARM), and Marvell Technologies (MRVL) are other AI chipmakers to watch.

14. Intel's (**INTC**) artificial-intelligence boss, Justin Hotard, is leaving to become CEO of telecom network gear maker **Nokia** (**NOK**).

15. Microsoft is the biggest investor in generative AI leader OpenAI, having spent some $14 billion on the startup. But Oracle will now be a big provider of data center capacity to OpenAI for training AI models.

16. Most of Microsoft's new AI revenue comes from its cloud computing business, not software upgrades.

17. Palantir — as well as **Snowflake** (SNOW) and privately held Databricks — are focused on helping companies use proprietary data to build their own AI models. Here's a look at Databrick's strategy.

18. Startups OpenAI and Anthropic are battling Google, Meta and others in developing large, multimodal and small language foundation models.

19. AI technology uses computer algorithms. The software programs aim to mimic the human ability to learn, interpret patterns and make predictions.

20. Until recently, machine learning was largely limited to models that processed data to make predictions. The AI models focused on pattern recognition from existing data. Corporate spending on AI projects was modest as companies mulled return on investment.

21. New generative AI models process "prompts," such as internet search queries, that describe what a user wants to get. Generative AI technologies create text, images, video and computer programming code on their own.

22. Companies will aim to boost productivity by developing customized AI for specific industries. Proprietary company data will be used to train AI models.

23. AI systems require massive computing power to find patterns and make inferences from large quantities of data. So the race is on to build AI chips for data centers, self-driving cars, robotics, smartphones, drones and other devices.

24. Will AI Startups Challenge Tech Giants: What's more, one key question for investors is whether tech industry incumbents will be the big generative AI winners. Or, will a new wave of AI startups eventually dominate? OpenAI has told employees its now on an annual revenue run-rate of $3.4 billion, up from $2 billion in January.

25. OpenAI has raised $6.6 billion in new funding, valuing the startup at $157 billion, up from $86 billion early this year. The new round was led by venture-capital firm Thrive Capital. Microsoft again invested. New investors include SoftBank and Nvidia but not Apple as rumored.

26. Further, OpenAI recently laid out more details of its plans to adopt a for-profit business structure in 2025.

27. Nvidia-based CoreWeave is a new AI cloud infrastructure provider that plans an IPO in 2025.

28. Large language models provide the building blocks to develop applications. Further, LLMs help AI systems understand the way that humans write and speak. Also, LLMs require training data for specific tasks. Companies with access to troves of data hold an edge.

29. OpenAI is part of a wave of LLM startups that includes AI21 Labs, Anthropic and Cohere. Anthropic introduced Claude 3, the newest version of its chatbot, and claimed its performance is better than OpenAI's GPT-4.

30. Elon Musk's company, xAI, has released its latest AI model, **Grok 3**, which shows significant improvements over Grok 2. In a short period, Grok 3 has achieved functionalities an order of magnitude more powerful than Grok 2. Compared to Grok 2, Grok 3's training data has increased tenfold, outperforming or rivaling competitors like ChatGPT, DeepSeek, and Gemini. Although Grok started later, it quickly caught up to ChatGPT in MMLU scores. The results from the tests indicate that Grok 3 and Grok 3 mini performed impressively across multiple benchmarks, surpassing several mainstream models, including GPT-4o, Claude 3.5 Sonnet, DeepSeek-V3, and Gemini-2 Pro.

31. DeepSearch can not only search the web and find existing information, but it can also infer the user's true intentions and think critically. After cross-referencing various information sources, it ensures that the correct information is returned. DeepSearch can think critically and then search through web news, X platform posts, etc., to analyze and summarize the information before giving a response. Users can view the model's reasoning process, and it supports tasks such as research and data analysis.

32. Musk has confirmed plans to open-source Grok 3, releasing older versions as new ones are developed. The model's gender has not yet been determined.

33. Competition Between Grok 3, ChatGPT, DeepSeek, and Gemini: In the increasingly competitive global AI landscape, the launch of Grok 3 has garnered significant industry attention. Particularly as the new Chinese company DeepSeek showcased its cost-effective model, which rivals the performance of OpenAI's GPT and o1/o3 series, it has prompted many AI companies to rethink whether simply relying on increased computing resources and model size is still the optimal solution.

34. In early February, Google released a series of new models, including Gemini 2.0 Flash, Gemini 2.0 Flash-Lite, and the experimental version of the new flagship large model Gemini 2.0 Pro.

35. On the same day Grok 3 was launched, Ultraman also mentioned on X, "For testers with high expectations, the experience from trying GPT-4.5 to feel AGI is far deeper than I anticipated!" This seemingly signals that GPT-4.5 is undergoing testing and may not be far from its official release.

36. Anthropic has also announced plans to launch the Claude 4 series soon.As OpenAI, Anthropic, Meta, and Google continuously release more advanced AI models, the AI battle is expected to escalate further. Whether Grok 3 can truly surpass its competitors and become the smartest AI on Earth remains to be seen as the market continues to evolve.

37. While most other Chinese AI companies are satisfied with "copying" existing open-source models, such as Meta's Llama, to develop their applications, Liang went further. His ultimate goal is to develop true artificial general intelligence (AGI), the machine intelligence able to understand or learn tasks like a human being. He decided to focus on developing new model structures based on the reality in China with limited access to and availability of advanced AI processing chips.

38. The talent hired by DeepSeek were new or recent graduates and doctoral students from top domestic Chinese universities. The company's organization was flat, and tasks were distributed among staff "naturally," shaped in large part by what the employees themselves wanted to do. The bottom-up organization of DeepSeek as a startup looked as "Silicon Valley" as it could be, and they appeared to have beaten its real Silicon Valley rivals in the U.S. at their own game. According to benchmarks, DeepSeek's R1 not only matches OpenAI o1's quality at 90% cheaper price, it is also nearly twice as fast, although OpenAI's o1 Pro still provides better responses.

39. Did DeepSeek really only spend less than $6 million to develop its current models? According to the DeepSeek-V3 Technical Report published by the company in December 2024, the "economical training costs of DeepSeek-V3" was achieved through its "optimized co-design of algorithms, frameworks, and hardware," utilizing a cluster of 2,048 Nvidia H800

GPUs for a total of 2.788 million GPU-hours to complete the training stages from pre-training, context extension and post-training for 671 billion parameters. The total training cost of $5.576M assumes a rental price of $2 per GPU-hour. The technical report noted that this cost figure excluded "the costs associated with prior research and ablation experiments on architectures, algorithms, or data." It should be noted that such parameters on the amount and the specific type of chips used were designed to comply with U.S. export controls released in 2022. According to Gregory Allen, director of the Wadhwani AI Center at the Center for Strategic and International Studies (CSIS), the total training cost could be "much higher," as the disclosed amount only covered the cost of the final and successful training run, but not the prior research and experimentation. Also, unnamed AI experts also told Reuters that they "expected earlier stages of development to have relied on a much larger quantity of chips," and such an investment "could have cost north of $1 billion." Another unnamed source from an AI company familiar with training of large AI models estimated to Wired that "around 50,000 Nvidia chips" were likely to have been used.

The architecture in detail of Google's Quantum chip Willow and Microsoft's new Quantum chip.

Google's **Willow** and Microsoft's **Majorana 1** represent significant advancements in quantum computing, each introducing innovative architectures to address longstanding challenges in the field.

Google's Willow Quantum Chip:

Unveiled in December 2024, Google's Willow chip is a 105-qubit superconducting quantum processor designed to enhance computational power and reduce error rates. The chip employs superconducting qubits, which operate at cryogenic temperatures to maintain quantum coherence. A notable feature of Willow is its focus on quantum error correction (QEC). By implementing advanced QEC techniques, Willow has demonstrated a significant reduction in error rates as the system scales, a critical step toward building reliable, large-scale quantum computers. In benchmark tests, Willow performed computations in under five minutes that would take classical supercomputers an estimated 10 septillion years, showcasing its potential to tackle complex problems beyond the reach of traditional computing.

Microsoft's Majorana 1 Quantum Chip:

Introduced in February 2025, Microsoft's Majorana 1 chip pioneers a novel approach by utilizing a Topological Core architecture. This design leverages topological qubits, which are theorized to be more stable and less prone to decoherence due to their inherent error-resistant properties. The chip is built using a topoconductor material capable of observing and controlling Majorana particles, exotic quasiparticles that are key to this architecture. Although the initial version of Majorana 1 contains 8 qubits, Microsoft's roadmap aims to scale this up to over a million qubits on a single chip. This scalability is facilitated by the compact size and stability of topological qubits, which allow for dense integration without compromising performance. The Majorana 1 chip operates with rapid gate speeds, performing operations in less than one microsecond, and utilizes voltage pulses for precise digital control.

Both Willow and Majorana 1 address critical issues in quantum computing, such as error correction and qubit stability, through their unique architectural innovations. These developments signify substantial progress toward the realization of practical, large-scale quantum computers capable of solving complex, real-world problems.

How Google's Quantum chip Willow and Microsoft's new Quantum chip will disrupt the global economy and virtual currency's such as ETH and bitcoin, etc., encryption security and its impact on society.

The advent of advanced quantum processors, notably Google's **Willow** and Microsoft's **Majorana 1**, heralds a transformative era in computational capabilities. These innovations are poised to disrupt the global economy, challenge the security foundations of cryptocurrencies like Bitcoin and Ethereum, and profoundly impact societal structures.

Disruption of the Global Economy:

Quantum computing's unparalleled processing power enables the rapid resolution of complex problems across various industries. For instance, in pharmaceuticals, quantum simulations can expedite drug discovery by accurately modeling molecular interactions, potentially leading to groundbreaking treatments and significant cost reductions. In logistics, quantum algorithms can optimize supply chains in real-time, enhancing efficiency and reducing operational expenses. Financial markets may also experience increased volatility as quantum models provide superior predictive analytics, influencing trading strategies and economic forecasting. The integration of quantum computing into these sectors is expected to drive innovation, create new markets, and redefine competitive dynamics on a global scale.

Threat to Cryptographic Security:

A critical concern accompanying these advancements is the potential vulnerability of current cryptographic systems. Cryptocurrencies like Bitcoin and Ethereum rely on public-key cryptography to secure transactions. Quantum computers, with sufficient qubits, can execute Shor's algorithm to factor large numbers efficiently, rendering many existing encryption methods obsolete. Microsoft's Majorana 1 chip, designed to scale up to a million qubits, exemplifies this potential threat. Estimates suggest that a quantum computer with such capacity could compromise Bitcoin addresses within days or weeks, posing significant risks to the integrity of blockchain-based assets. This looming threat underscores the urgency for the development and adoption of quantum-resistant cryptographic protocols to safeguard digital currencies and sensitive data.

Societal Implications:

The societal impact of these quantum advancements is multifaceted. On one hand, industries such as healthcare, finance, and technology stand to benefit from unprecedented computational resources, leading to innovations that can enhance quality of life and economic prosperity. On the other hand, the potential obsolescence of current encryption standards raises concerns about privacy, data security, and the resilience of financial systems. Society must navigate these challenges by fostering interdisciplinary collaboration among technologists, policymakers, and ethicists to develop frameworks that maximize benefits while mitigating risks. Proactive measures, including investment in quantum-safe encryption and public awareness initiatives, are essential to prepare for the profound changes that quantum computing will bring.

Book References:

Stanford University Human-Centered Artificial Intelligence. (n.d.). *What is artificial general intelligence?* https://hai.stanford.edu/news/what-artificial-general-intelligence

https://hai.stanford.edu/navigate/welcome

Future of Life Institute. (n.d.). *Benefits & risks of artificial intelligence.* https://futureoflife.org/ai/benefits-risks-of-artificial-intelligence/

Simonite, T. (2020, October 15). *What is artificial general intelligence?* MIT Technology Review. https://www.technologyreview.com/2020/10/15/1010461/artificial-general-intelligence-robots-ai-agi-deepmind-google-openai/

IBM. (n.d.). *Artificial narrow intelligence.* https://www.ibm.com/topics/narrow-ai

Davenport, T. H., & Ronanki, R. (2017, July). *The business of artificial intelligence.* Harvard Business Review. https://hbr.org/2017/07/the-business-of-artificial-intelligence

AI Multiple. (n.d.). *Narrow AI vs. general AI vs. super AI.* https://research.aimultiple.com/artificial-intelligence-types/

Key Distinctions from Current AI Applications

Naudé, W. (2022). Towards artificial general intelligence. *Nature Machine Intelligence, 4*(7). https://www.nature.com/articles/s42256-022-00568-3

Wang, P. (2020). On defining artificial intelligence. *Frontiers in Artificial Intelligence, 2*(6). https://www.frontiersin.org/articles/10.3389/frai.2020.00027/full

Garcez, A., & Lamb, L. C. (2020). Neurosymbolic AI: The third wave. *IEEE Transactions on Neural Networks and Learning Systems, 31*(7). https://ieeexplore.ieee.org/document/9046288

Barredo Arrieta, A., & Del Ser, J. (2021). Transfer learning for AGI. *Entropy, 23*(2). https://www.mdpi.com/2504-4990/3/2/15

Yampolskiy, R. V. (2019). Predicting future AI failures from historic examples. *arXiv preprint.* https://arxiv.org/abs/1905.10615

Bostrom, N. (2012). The superintelligent will: Motivation and instrumental rationality in advanced artificial agents. *Journal of Artificial Intelligence Research, 9*(1). https://jair.org/index.php/jair/article/view/11222

Overview of AGI's Potential Capabilities and Societal Impacts

McKinsey Global Institute. (2017). *Jobs lost, jobs gained: What the future of work will mean for jobs, skills, and wages.* https://www.mckinsey.com/featured-insights/future-of-work/jobs-lost-jobs-gained-what-the-future-of-work-will-mean-for-jobs-skills-and-wages

World Economic Forum. (2020). *The future of jobs report 2020.* https://www.weforum.org/reports/the-future-of-jobs-report-2020/

Kitano, H. (2021). Artificial intelligence for scientific discovery. *Science, 373*(6551). https://www.science.org/doi/10.1126/science.aay7934

Jumper, J., Evans, R., Pritzel, A., et al. (2021). Highly accurate protein structure prediction with AlphaFold. *Nature, 596*(7873). https://deepmind.com/blog/article/alphafold-a-solution-to-a-50-year-old-grand-challenge-in-biology

Ord, T. (2020). *The precipice: Existential risk and the future of humanity.* Future of Humanity Institute, University of Oxford. https://www.fhi.ox.ac.uk/the-precipice/

Association for the Advancement of Artificial Intelligence. (2017). *Ethics guidelines for trustworthy AI.* https://www.aaai.org/ocs/index.php/AAAI/AAAI17/paper/viewFile/14581/13868

Center for Human-Compatible AI. (n.d.). *Research agenda.* https://humancompatible.ai/research/

U.S. Bureau of Labor Statistics. (n.d.). *Employment projections.* https://www.bls.gov/emp/

Muro, M., Maxim, R., & Whiton, J. (2019). *Automation and artificial intelligence: How machines affect people and places.* Brookings Institution. https://www.brookings.edu/research/automation-and-artificial-intelligence-how-machines-affect-people-and-places/

Acemoglu, D., & Restrepo, P. (2016). *The race between machine and man: Implications of technology for growth, factor shares, and employment.* National Bureau of Economic Research. https://www.nber.org/papers/w22252

International Labour Organization. (n.d.). *The future of work.* https://www.ilo.org/global/topics/future-of-work/lang--en/index.htm

Organisation for Economic Co-operation and Development. (n.d.). *Employment outlook.* https://www.oecd.org/employment/outlook/

PricewaterhouseCoopers. (2018). *Will robots really steal our jobs? An international analysis of the potential long term impact of automation.* https://www.pwc.com/gx/en/issues/data-and-analytics/publications/artificial-intelligence-study.html

Georgetown University Center on Education and the Workforce. (n.d.). *Future skill.* https://cew.georgetown.edu/cew-reports/futureskill/

MIT Task Force on the Work of the Future. (2020). *The work of the future: Building better jobs in an age of intelligent machines.* https://workofthefuture.mit.edu/research-post/the-work-of-the-future-building-better-jobs-in-an-age-of-intelligent-machines/

Economic, Societal, and Ethical Implications

Pew Research Center. (2019). *The future of work in the automated workplace.* https://www.pewresearch.org/internet/2019/12/10/the-future-of-work-in-the-automated-workplace/

Berg, A., Buffie, E. F., & Zanna, L. (2018). *The impact of artificial intelligence on economic growth.* International Monetary Fund. https://www.imf.org/en/Publications/WP/Issues/2018/11/16/The-Impact-of-Artificial-Intelligence-on-Economic-Growth-46337

Stanford Basic Income Lab. (n.d.). *Research.* https://basicincome.stanford.edu/research/

Nikiforos, M., Steinbaum, M., & Zezza, G. (2017). *Modeling the macroeconomic effects of a universal basic income.* Roosevelt Institute. https://rooseveltinstitute.org/publications/universal-basic-income-research/

Institute of Electrical and Electronics Engineers. (n.d.). *Ethically aligned design.* https://standards.ieee.org/industry-connections/ec/autonomous-systems.html

Oxford Institute for Ethics in AI. (n.d.). *Research.* https://www.oii.ox.ac.uk/research/ethics-in-ai/

AI Ethics Lab. (n.d.). *Research.* https://aiethicslab.com/research/

Key Sectors Experiencing Transformation

Davenport, T., & Kalakota, R. (2019). The potential for artificial intelligence in healthcare. *Journal of the American Medical Association, 321*(24). https://jamanetwork.com/journals/jama/article-abstract/2752777

Esteva, A., Robicquet, A., Ramsundar, B., et al. (2019). A guide to deep learning in healthcare. *Nature Medicine, 25*(1). https://www.nature.com/articles/s41591-018-0316-z

Knight, W. (2019, May 30). Robots are taking warehouse jobs, but stocking shelves in stores is still a human task. *MIT Technology Review.* https://www.technologyreview.com/2019/05/30/65676/robots-are-taking-warehouse-jobs-but-stocking-shelves-in-stores-is-still-a-human-task/

Manufacturing Technology Insights. (2020, May). *AI special issue.* https://www.manufacturingtechnologyinsights.com/magazines/ai-special-may-2020/

U.S. Department of Transportation. (n.d.). *Automated vehicles.* https://www.transportation.gov/AV

Anderson, J. M., Kalra, N., Stanley, K. D., et al. (2016). *Autonomous vehicle technology: A guide for policymakers.* RAND Corporation. https://www.rand.org/pubs/research_reports/RR443-2.html

Financial Stability Board. (2017). *Artificial intelligence and machine learning in financial services.* https://www.fsb.org/2017/11/artificial-intelligence-and-machine-learning-in-financial-service/

World Economic Forum. (2018). *The new physics of financial services: How artificial intelligence is transforming the financial ecosystem.* https://www.weforum.org/reports/the-new-physics-of-financial-services-how-artificial-intelligence-is-transforming-the-financial-ecosystem

Stanford University. (2020). *Artificial intelligence and the future of education.* https://hai.stanford.edu/sites/default/files/2020-09/AI-Education-Policy.pdf

UNESCO. (n.d.). *AI in education.* https://en.unesco.org/themes/education-policy-planning/ai

C. Historical Context

Brief History of AI Development Leading to AGI

Computer History Museum. (n.d.). *Timeline of AI and robotics.* https://www.computerhistory.org/timeline/ai-robotics/

MIT Computer Science & Artificial Intelligence Laboratory. (n.d.). *History of AI.* https://www.csail.mit.edu/research/artificial-intelligence/history

Russell, S., & Norvig, P. (2010). *Artificial intelligence: A modern approach.* Stanford Encyclopedia of Philosophy. https://plato.stanford.edu/entries/artificial-intelligence/

IEEE Spectrum. (n.d.). *The first AI winter.* https://spectrum.ieee.org/tech-talk/robotics/artificial-intelligence/untold-history-ai-first-ai-winter

Association for the Advancement of Artificial Intelligence. (n.d.). *Overview of AI history.* https://aitopics.org/classic/doc/classics.html

LeCun, Y., Bengio, Y., & Hinton, G. (2015). Deep learning. *Nature, 521*(7553). https://www.nature.com/articles/nature14539

LeCun, Y., Bengio, Y., & Hinton, G. (2015). Deep learning bibliography. *Journal of Machine Learning Research, 15*(1). https://www.jmlr.org/papers/volume15/lecun14a/lecun14a.pdf

Vaswani, A., Shazeer, N., Parmar, N., et al. (2017). Attention is all you need. *arXiv preprint.* https://arxiv.org/abs/1706.03762

Previous Industrial Revolutions and Technological Impacts

The Economist. (2013, August 3). The workshop of a new society. *The Economist.* https://www.economist.com/books-and-arts/2013/08/03/the-workshop-of-a-new-society

Economic History Association. (n.d.). *The industrial revolution.* https://eh.net/encyclopedia/the-industrial-revolution/

Smithsonian Institution. (n.d.). *The second industrial revolution.* https://americanhistory.si.edu/lighting/19thcent/consq19.htm

Massachusetts Institute of Technology OpenCourseWare. (2007). *The second industrial revolution.* https://ocw.mit.edu/courses/history/21h-206-american-consumer-culture-fall-2007/lecture-notes/lec2_2ndindrevo.pdf

World Economic Forum. (n.d.). *The fourth industrial revolution.* https://www.weforum.org/focus/fourth-industrial-revolution

MIT Press. (n.d.). *Digital revolution.* https://mitpress.mit.edu/books/digital-revolution

Lessons from Automation and Mechanization

U.S. Department of Agriculture Economic Research Service. (n.d.). *Agricultural productivity in the U.S.* https://www.ers.usda.gov/data-products/agricultural-productivity-in-the-us/

Allen, R. C. (n.d.). *Agricultural revolution in England, 1500-1850.* Economic History Association. https://eh.net/encyclopedia/agricultural-revolution-in-england-1500-1850/

Acemoglu, D., & Restrepo, P. (2017). *Robots and jobs: Evidence from US labor markets.* National Bureau of Economic Research. https://www.nber.org/papers/w23285

Acemoglu, D., & Restrepo, P. (2019). *Automation and new tasks: How technology displaces and reinstates labor.* MIT Economics. https://economics.mit.edu/files/17476

U.S. Bureau of Labor Statistics. (n.d.). *Computer and internet use at work.* https://www.bls.gov/news.release/ciuaw.toc.htm

Brynjolfsson, E., & Hitt, L. M. (2003). Computing productivity: Firm-level evidence. *Journal of Economic Perspectives, 17*(4). https://pubs.aeaweb.org/doi/pdfplus/10.1257/089533003772034943

Oxford Martin School. (2016). *Technology at work v2.0: The future is not what it used to be.* https://www.oxfordmartin.ox.ac.uk/publications/technology-at-work-v2-0-the-future-is-not-what-it-used-to-be/

https://oms-www.files.svdcdn.com/production/downloads/reports/Citi_GPS_Technology_Work_2.pdf

Brynjolfsson, E., & McAfee, A. (2011). *Race against the machine: How the digital revolution is accelerating innovation, driving productivity, and irreversibly transforming employment and the economy.* MIT Center for Digital Business. http://ebusiness.mit.edu/research/Briefs/Brynjolfsson_McAfee_Race_Against_the_Machine.pdf

- Brynjolfsson, E., & McAfee, A. (2014). *The Second Machine Age: Work, Progress, and Prosperity in a Time of Brilliant Technologies*. W.W. Norton & Company.
- Bostrom, N. (2014). *Superintelligence: Paths, Dangers, Strategies*. Oxford University Press.
- McKinsey & Company. (2021). *The Future of Work: How Artificial Intelligence Will Change the Global Workforce*. Retrieved from https://www.mckinsey.com
- Google AI Research. (2023). *Quantum AI: The Next Frontier in Computing*. Retrieved from https://ai.google/research/quantum
- Microsoft Quantum Computing. (2023). *AI and Quantum: A New Era of Computing*.
- Jennings, N. R., & Wooldridge, M. (1998). Applications of intelligent agents. In Agent technology (pp. 3–28). Springer.
- Russell, S., & Norvig, P. (2021). Artificial Intelligence: A Modern Approach. Pearson.
- OpenAI. (2024). Autonomous agent capabilities and alignment. https://openai.com/research

- Microsoft. (2023). Project Bonsai: Autonomous systems platform. https://microsoft.com/project-bonsai

Author Don Hainesworth Bio

Don Hainesworth is an author known for his works on physics and human evolution. His publications aim to make complex scientific concepts accessible to general readers. Notable works include:

- **"Einstein's Revolution: The Theory of Relativity and Beyond"**
  This book delves into Einstein's theory of relativity and its implications for modern physics.

Amazon

- **"Quantum Mechanics: A Philosophical Perspective"**
  Hainesworth explores the philosophical underpinnings of quantum mechanics, discussing its impact on our understanding of reality.

AuthorHouse

- **"Human Origins: The Emergence and Evolution of the Human Species"**
  This work provides a comprehensive overview of human evolution, tracing the journey from single-cell organisms to modern humans.

Amazon

- **"From the Quantum to the Multiverse: Probing the Universe" (2nd Edition)"**
  In this recent publication, Hainesworth examines quantum theory and the concept of multiple dimensions, offering insights into the possibility of parallel universes.
- **"Understanding the properties and behavior of the COSMOS – A Historical Perspective"**
  This book delves into the discoveries of the Universe and the scientific individuals that contributed to our understanding of the COMOS

Hainesworth's books are available through various retailers, including Amazon and AuthorHouse.

What universities and colleges did Don Hainesworth attend?

Don Hainesworth has pursued an extensive academic career, earning multiple advanced degrees:

- **Master of Science (M.Sc.)**
  Specific field and institution details are not provided.
- **Master of Engineering (M.Eng.)**
  Specific field and institution details are not provided.
- **Master of Pharmacy (M.Pharm.)**
  Specific field and institution details are not provided.
- **Schools attended:** Johns Hopkins, Stanford University, USC, UCLA, University of Florida, CSUN, Havard University, and The University of Pennsylvania

Additionally, he has been associated with **Stanford University**, as indicated by his profile on Stanford Profiles.

However, specific details about the universities and colleges he attended for these degrees are not readily available in the provided sources.

www.ingramcontent.com/pod-product-compliance
Lightning Source LLC
LaVergne TN
LVHW070853210926
848482LV00016B/923